The Nice Girl Syndrome

To Carrie —

I'm not even sure if this
book is any good or not,
but I do hope the incentive
behind it helps you reflect
¿ realize your true value.
You have so much to offer the
world and only get one life
to do so. You, as well as
every other human being deserve
to fill those days with happiness,
to make choices, (even though
they may be difficult), on who
is to surround yourself with —
the type of people worthy of
your time so that both you
yourself and they can reach

your fullest potentials. College is ending soon, and I know we will both be heading on our own separate paths, but I also know our sails will never be far apart—they are too entertwined and too much alike. When you feel pain it affects me, and maybe that has the same affect on you...

Anyways, please, please, please never settle—whether it is with guys, jobs, opportunities, etc. Our sad but beautiful fate as mortals is that we are not infinite—something I am still trying to wrap my head around. We each have a limited # of days, so please fill yours with people and situations worthy of that time. I know not every day will be easy, but I know in my heart that if we keep on striving we reach

our fullest potential eventually.
The potential you have is so
great — and that is just what
I have witnessed! Think of
what you will accomplish
in the future!

The Nice Girl
Syndrome

*Stop Being Manipulated and Abused—
and Start Standing Up for Yourself*

BEVERLY ENGEL

Remember —
never settle.

much love,
Caroline

WILEY
John Wiley & Sons, Inc.

Published by John Wiley & Sons, Inc., Hoboken, New Jersey

Published simultaneously in Canada

For general information about our other products and services, please contact our Customer Care Department within the United States at (800) 762-2974, outside the United States at (317) 572-3993 or fax (317) 572-4002.

Wiley also publishes its books in a variety of electronic formats. Some content that appears in print may not be available in electronic books. For more information about Wiley products, visit our web site at www.wiley.com.

Library of Congress Cataloging-in-Publication Data:

Engel, Beverly.
  The nice girl syndrome : stop being manipulated and abused—and start standing up for yourself / Beverly Engel.
     p. cm.
  Includes bibliographical references and index.
  ISBN 978-0-470-17938-3 (cloth)
  ISBN 978-0-470-57990-9 (paper)
  1. Women—Life skills guides. 2. Women—Psychology. 3. Self-confidence. 4. Self-esteem. 5. Psychological abuse—Popular works. I. Title.
  HQ1221.E54 2008
  155.6'33—dc22   2008008382

Printed in the United States of America

10   9   8   7   6   5   4

This book is dedicated to the many women in the world who still believe they have to be nice in order to be loved, accepted, taken care of, and safe. It is also for all the women's advocates who work so diligently to help women understand that it is better to be strong than to be nice.

Contents

Part Three   From Nice Girl to Strong Woman

Acknowledgments

Once again, I wish to thank my agents, Stedman Mays and Mary Tahan, and my editor at Wiley, Tom Miller. Thanks also to production editor Lisa Burstiner, who always does a wonderful job of editing my work. I appreciate your thoroughness and your restraint. I am extremely grateful to all of you for making it possible for me to have a second life in publishing. This will be our eighth book together, and I think we make a great team!

My heartfelt gratitude goes to the women researchers who gave this book its backbone: Carol Gilligan, Anne Campbell, Susan Faludi, Mary Pipher, and Rachel Simmons.

I also wish to acknowledge the work of Laurel Mellin, who has created an incredible program for helping people to rid themselves of false beliefs. It is her concept of "positive and powerful statements" that I included in this book. I highly recommend her program and her book *The Pathway: Follow the Road to Health and Happiness*.

Last but certainly not least, I want to thank all the Nice Girls I have worked with throughout the years. Your courage and determination to become Strong Women inspired me to write this book.

Introduction

In this day and age, you would think that women would have learned enough about assertiveness, boundaries, and codependency that they wouldn't continue to be used and abused. There certainly are enough books on the subjects. So why is it that women continue to be victimized and taken advantage of by lovers, partners, family members, friends, and co-workers?

The main reason certainly lies in the fact that we still allow abusive men to mistreat women. Although there has been some progress when it comes to exposing and treating abusers, there are still far too many men who believe they have the right to abuse "their" women.

We've come a long way since the time when men believed that their wives and daughters were their property and they had the right to treat them any way they saw fit. But there needs to be more pressure put on abusive men to get the treatment they need.

In spite of a great deal of public education, we are still dealing with a huge problem when it comes to the abuse of women. Statistics tell us that women continue to be abused in record numbers. For example:

- The American Medical Association estimates that over 4 million women are victims of severe assaults by boyfriends and husbands each year.

- Around the world, at least 1 in every 3 women has been beaten, coerced into sex, or otherwise abused in her lifetime.

- Nearly one-third of American women (31 percent) report being physically or sexually abused by a husband or a boyfriend at some point in their lives.

- Approximately 1 in 5 female high school students report being physically and/or sexually abused by a dating partner.

- Three in 4 women (76 percent) who reported that they had been raped and/or physically assaulted since age eighteen said that a current or former husband, cohabitating partner, or date committed the assault.
- Nearly one-fifth of women (18 percent) reported experiencing a completed or attempted rape at some time in their lives.
- Annually in the United States, 503,485 women are stalked by an intimate partner. Seventy-eight percent of stalking victims are women.

In addition to there not being enough done to expose and treat abusive men, I propose that another reason women continue to be victimized is that they are too nice for their own good. This niceness attracts the wrong kind of people and sends the message that these women are easy targets to be taken advantage of, controlled, and even emotionally, physically, and sexually abused. It also prevents women from standing up for themselves and keeps them in relationships that are unhealthy or abusive.

During my long career as a psychotherapist, I've often heard clients describe painful, shocking, and even bizarre experiences. After thirty years of practice, specializing in abuse, I have become somewhat hardened to just how cruel we human beings can be to one another. And yet there is something that I never seem to get used to: how often women put up with unacceptable, often horrible treatment from others, especially men. Every time I hear a woman describe the mistreatment, abuse, even sadistic cruelty that she has endured, it saddens me. Although I know the answers, I often find myself thinking, "Why does she put up with this?" Even more upsetting to me is that often these women are worried about their abusive partners. "I don't know what he'll do without me," they frequently respond when we talk about their getting out of the abusive relationship. Or, "I know that my leaving will kill him. He can't stand to be alone." In the midst of their own personal crises, they are more worried about their abusive partners than they are about themselves.

I've written numerous books, many about recovering from some form of abuse. In most of those books, in addition to offering survivors advice and strategies on how to cope with or get away from an abuser, I have asked them to look at their part in the situation.

Always stressing that I do not mean to blame the victim in any way, I encourage them to look for the reasons they have stayed in an abusive relationship and why they chose an abuser in the first place. In this book, I will ask victims and survivors to go one step further—to look for the roots of their Nice Girl behavior.

It is my contention that Nice Girl behavior sets women up to be misused and abused. This does not mean that women cause men to become abusive. It does not mean that women are masochists. What it does mean is that by being too nice, women send a strong message to those who already have a tendency to use and abuse. The message is: "My need to be seen as nice (or sweet or innocent) is more powerful than my instinct to protect myself."

The hard truth is that women cannot afford to be Nice Girls. It simply is not safe. Too many people (women as well as men) take advantage of any weakness they find in another person. Being too nice is certainly viewed as a weakness.

In this book, I write about the difference between Nice Girls and what I call Strong Women. I teach women how to put aside their Nice Girl thinking and behavior and to instead adopt what I call Strong Women thinking and behavior. Although not every Nice Girl gets raped or is emotionally, verbally, or physically abused in her relationships, every Nice Girl is putting herself at risk by continuing to believe and act as she does. Nice Girls tend to put up with inappropriate or abusive behavior, to minimize the damage they are experiencing, and to make excuses for their partners. *The Nice Girl Syndrome* will help women to stop being nice and start being strong, to stand up for themselves, and to refuse to be treated in abusive ways.

The primary audience for *The Nice Girl Syndrome* is women who have been or are currently being emotionally, verbally, or physically abused by their partners; women who have been raped or date-raped; and women who are being or have been stalked by an intimate partner. But nearly every woman has some Nice Girl still left in her. While younger women (ages eighteen to thirty) will be especially attracted to this book, women thirty-one and older will also find the book interesting, provocative, and helpful. Unfortunately, Nice Girls don't tend to grow out of this behavior all that easily.

This book is not about codependency or "relationship addiction." The self-help plan for codependency, as outlined by CODA

(Codependents Anonymous) and books such as Robin Norwood's *Women Who Love Too Much* is for women to *surrender*. My treatment program, on the other hand, has more to do with the notion of standing up for your rights.

Susan Faludi, in her groundbreaking book *Backlash: The Undeclared War against American Women*, noted that instead of encouraging women to become stronger, to defend themselves, and to challenge men to change, Norwood recommended that women "build [their] willingness to surrender," and "let go of self-will." Taking the initiative to improve one's situation was not part of the Norwood plan. Instead, she advised letting go of "the determination to make things happen." She further explained, "You must accept the fact that you may not know what is best in a given situation."

You will not hear anything like this in my book. In fact, you will hear the opposite. I encourage women to trust their instincts more and to never allow anyone to tell them that they do not know what is best for them. I will encourage them to become more assertive, not more passive.

Norwood's plan, modeled on Alcoholics Anonymous's 12-step program, advised women seeking the source of their pain to refrain from looking beyond themselves, a habit she calls "blaming." My plan encourages women to stop taking all the blame for the problems in their relationships and to begin to recognize that often they are putting up with intolerable behavior from others. Blaming an abusive partner, for example, in the interest of freeing yourself from an intolerable situation can be a healthy thing if it means that you stop blaming yourself. I encourage women to stop blaming themselves and place their righteous anger where it belongs: on the people, past and present, who have mistreated or abused them.

While I do address some of the same issues that books on people-pleasing do, such as discomfort with and fear of anger, hostility, conflict, and confrontation, I also name and focus on other factors that contribute to women's victimization, such as the long history of female oppression, feeling powerless and helpless, being too gullible, being in denial about the current dangers in our society, being in denial about one's own dark side, having an overly strong need to be fair, and having religious and spiritual beliefs that set one up to be used and abused.

In addition to covering the psychological reasons for niceness (guilt, shame, low self-esteem, fear of confrontation, fear of rejection, intense fear of being alone), I also focus heavily on the *societal* reasons, such as the fact that women and girls are *conditioned* to become Nice Girls.

I focus specifically on the *beliefs and attitudes* that set women up to be used and abused. I offer a specific program for unearthing and discarding these deeply buried false beliefs and attitudes and replacing them with the truth. And I offer remedies—exercises and steps—women can take to heal themselves of the brainwashing that created these false beliefs in the first place. Finally, I offer an empowerment challenge that will help women develop what I call the four C's: confidence, competence, conviction, and courage.

In *The Nice Girl Syndrome*, women will learn that they can be kind without sacrificing their souls and that they can give people the benefit of the doubt without being pushovers. Most important, they will learn they can remain feminine without giving up their power.

Most women don't want to continue their Nice Girl act. It has become too cumbersome. It feels dishonest. It keeps them from finding out what they really feel and who they really are. In the following chapters you will learn how and why women have been programmed to hide their true feelings behind a mask of sweetness and niceness. By learning the causes of the Nice Girl syndrome you will be taking the first step toward dismantling the false beliefs that are the underpinnings of the Nice Girl syndrome.

PART ONE

STRONG WOMEN AREN'T NICE

STRONG WOMEN
AGAINST TYPE

1

The High Price of Being Too Nice

When one is pretending, the entire body revolts.

—ANAÏS NIN

A re you a Nice Girl? Do people often take advantage of your patience, compassion, and generosity? Are you constantly let down because other people don't treat you as well as you treat them? Do you constantly give others the benefit of the doubt, only to be disappointed when they don't come through? Do you tend to give other people too many chances? Is being too nice becoming a burden? If you answered yes to some or all of these questions, not only are you not alone but you are in the majority. There are millions of other Nice Girls worldwide who think and feel exactly as you do. In fact, it is safe to say that every woman has some Nice Girl in her. Here are just a few examples from my practice.

Heather's boyfriend had an old car that continually broke down. She worried about his having to drive his old clunker into the city every day to work, so she let him drive her car. After all, she rationalized, she didn't have to go as far to work and could easily take the bus. One day, Heather went out to her car only to find that a tire boot had been put on it. It turned out that her boyfriend had been getting tickets and then not paying for them. But this wasn't the worst part of the story. Instead of realizing that her boyfriend was not responsible enough to drive her car, Heather allowed him to continue to do so. Two months later, he totaled her car. The insurance company paid her only for what the car was currently worth, which wasn't enough for her to buy a new car. Did Heather's boyfriend help her pay for a new car? No. Did he even agree to drive her to work until she got a new car? No; he said it would make him late for work. Most important, did Heather say anything to him about his irresponsibility and inconsideration? No.

Mandy's husband, Jason, puts her down a lot. He corrects her whenever she mispronounces a word. He rolls his eyes in exasperation whenever she has a hard time figuring out how appliances work. He even makes disparaging remarks about her in front of other people. Mandy's friends tell her that Jason is a jerk and shouldn't treat her like that, but she explains that that is just the way he is. She knows Jason really loves her. He gets like that when he's stressed or tired.

Whenever Gwen's boyfriend, Ron, drinks too much, he starts treating her very disrespectfully in public. He talks loudly to others about how "stacked" Gwen is and what a great ass she has. He touches her inappropriately in front of others. And worst of all, he encourages other men to flirt with and dance with her. Gwen, a rather shy person, is very embarrassed and uncomfortable with all this. She quietly tells Ron to stop these behaviors, but her request has no effect on him. So instead of getting up and walking out, she just silently continues to take it for the rest of the evening.

Carolyn didn't like the way her manager at work looked at her or the fact that he often told her off-color jokes. She wondered if she had given him the wrong idea, so she started dressing more conservatively. Nothing changed. She thought of saying something to him, but she was afraid that he would be insulted, which could cause even more problems at work.

Heather, Mandy, Gwen, and Carolyn are all Nice Girls. Like many women, they are afraid to speak their minds either out of fear of hurting someone's feelings or out of fear of being rejected or hurt themselves. Unfortunately, they almost always end up paying quite a price for their silence. Heather lost her car to an irresponsible, uncaring boyfriend; Carolyn was constantly being sexually harassed; and the self-esteem of Mandy and Gwen is constantly being diminished.

What Is a Nice Girl?

Being a Nice Girl doesn't necessarily have anything to do with morals. Monica Lewinsky was a Nice Girl because she was naive enough to believe that President Bill Clinton loved her and was actually going to leave Hillary for her. She was a Nice Girl because she put his needs ahead of her own and was willing to continue lying for him, even after they were caught, and because she kept hoping they had a future together even when it was clear he had dumped her.

Neither does being a Nice Girl necessarily have anything to do with being kind or generous or respectful. Oprah Winfrey is all those things, but I don't believe anyone would describe her as being "nice." As warm as she is, she also sets very clear boundaries, letting people know what she will or will not put up with. And she is a person you wouldn't want to cross.

A Nice Girl is more concerned about what others think of her than she is about what she thinks of herself. Being a Nice Girl means that a woman is more concerned about other people's feelings than she is about her own. And it means she is more concerned about giving people the benefit of the doubt than she is about trusting her own perceptions.

According to the dictionary, synonyms for the word *nice* include *careful, pleasant, subtle, agreeable, likable, delightful, good, admirable, pleasing*. These words describe a Nice Girl to a T. In fact, many Nice Girls have an investment in being perceived in all of these ways. But I also think of other words when I think of the word *nice*, namely *compliant, passive, wishy-washy*, and *phony*.

Nice Girls are compliant; they do what they are told. They've learned that it is easier to just do what someone asks than to risk an argument. Nice girls are passive; they let things happen. They are often too afraid to stand up for themselves. They are walking door-mats who are easily manipulated and controlled. Nice Girls are wishy-washy. Because they are so afraid of confrontation, they say one thing one time and another thing another time. They want to please everyone all the time, and because of this they agree with one person and then turn right around and agree with someone else who has the exact opposite belief. Because they are afraid of telling others how they really feel, Nice Girls can be phony; they pretend a lot. They pretend they like someone when they don't. They pretend they want to be somewhere when they don't.

I realize that it may sound harsh to call someone phony—or compliant or passive or wishy-washy, for that matter. But I prefer to tell it the way it is, and in this book I am going to pump it up a notch or two because Nice Girls can also be something else—stubborn.

Many Nice Girls firmly believe that their way of operating is the right way. They are convinced that it works for them. And they tend to think they are taking the moral high ground and that others could benefit from being more like them. I am going to be firm also, because I know that for some of you it's going to be an uphill battle to get you to let go of your Nice Girl mentality.

This doesn't mean that I don't have compassion for those who are stuck in the Nice Girl syndrome, because I do. I understand all the reasons that you act as you do. I understand that it is not your fault. I understand that due to cultural conditioning, parental messages, and childhood experiences, those of you with the Nice Girl syndrome are simply doing what you have been conditioned or taught to do. I understand because I have been a Nice Girl myself.

How Big a Problem Is the Nice Girl Syndrome?

Surely in this day and age we must be talking about only a small number of women, right? Unfortunately, we are not. There are far more Nice Girls out there than you can imagine. Even the most empowered women have some Nice Girl in them.

Most women have tolerated unacceptable behavior from friends, family, or lovers for far too long in their attempts to be understanding, tolerant, and compassionate. We've all known women who are too nice for their own good. When someone does something to them that is inconsiderate, offensive, or even cruel, instead of getting angry they try to "understand" the other person. They spend more time asking why the person did what was done than in telling the other person how unacceptable his or her actions were.

If we didn't have so many Nice Girls, the rate of domestic violence and emotional abuse would be much lower than it is. We would not have so many women who stand by while their children are being emotionally, physically, or even sexually abused by their husbands and boyfriends. We would not have so many women staying in relationships in which they are being manipulated and taken advantage of. And we would not have so many women remaining silent when they are being sexually harassed, date-raped, or sexually pressured by their partners.

Is This Book for You?

This book is for all women who have yet to learn that if they don't take care of themselves, no one else will. It is for every woman who puts her own needs aside on a regular basis to either attract or keep a man. And it is for all the women who are beginning to learn that being nice doesn't pay off in the long run. Most especially, it is for all the women who are currently being emotionally, verbally, or physically abused.

If you are uncertain whether you are a Nice Girl, the following questionnaire will help you decide.

QUESTIONNAIRE: ARE YOU A NICE GIRL?

1. Do you have a difficult time asserting yourself with service people? (For example, sending a plate of food back, telling a salesperson you are not interested.)

2. Do you get talked into things, including buying things, because you can't say no?

3. Are you overly concerned about what people think of you?

4. Is it overly important to you that people like you?

5. Are you afraid to say how you really feel out of fear of making someone angry?

6. Do you apologize too much or too often?

7. Do you have friends or acquaintances you don't really like or have much in common with but feel obligated to continue seeing?

8. Do you often say yes to invitations because you don't want the person to feel rejected?

9. Do you tend to give in because it makes you feel selfish if you refuse to help someone?

10. Are you afraid people will dislike you if you're not cooperative?

11. Do you have trouble speaking up as soon as something or someone is unfair to you?

12. Do you hesitate telling someone that he or she has hurt your feelings or made you angry because you don't want him or her to feel bad?

13. Do you avoid telling someone he or she has upset you because you don't think it will do any good or will only cause a big problem between you?

14. Do you have people in your life who take advantage of you?

15. Do you often take the blame for things just to avoid an argument or to avoid rejection or abandonment?

16. Do you often make excuses for people's poor behavior, telling yourself that they didn't mean it or they didn't know better?

17. Do you avoid conflict or confrontation at all costs?

18. Do you get a terrible feeling when someone is angry with you?

19. Do you give someone the benefit of the doubt even when others tell you this person is trouble?

20. Do you give people another chance even when they continue with the same hurtful or inappropriate behavior?

21. Do you tell yourself that you don't have a right to complain about a person's behavior if you've ever been guilty of the same behavior?

22. Are you attracted to bad boys or people with a large dark side?

23. Do you strongly believe in being fair even when other people are treating you unfairly?

If you answered yes to two or more of these questions, you have some Nice Girl in you no matter how assertive, successful, or self-actualized you think you are. This book will help you to shed whatever vestiges of niceness you still have.

If you answered yes to more than five of these questions, you still have some work to do in terms of changing the way you view yourself in the world.

If you answered yes to more than ten of these questions, you have an extreme version of the Nice Girl syndrome and will need to do some serious work to rid yourself of the negative and false beliefs that are basically dictating your life.

You Cannot Afford to Be a Nice Girl

Why should you let go of your Nice Girl thinking and acting? Women today simply cannot afford to be Nice Girls. What do I mean by this? First and foremost, Nice Girls are far more likely to become victimized—emotionally, physically, and sexually—than are those who are not so nice.

For example, Karen agreed to go out with a man from work because she felt sorry for him. "I didn't like him, but he kept asking me out and I felt bad about constantly turning him down. He seemed so awkward around women. I thought it would be nice if I offered to make him a nice home-cooked meal." That night, after dinner, the man from work raped Karen. Not only did she blame herself for being so stupid as to invite him to her home, but she didn't report it. "I was just too embarrassed. I didn't want everyone at work to find out about it." And so every workday, Karen lives in fear that she will run into the man who raped her.

Karen's niceness had actually put her life in jeopardy. She allowed her concern for someone else to blind her to the dangers of dealing with a stranger. Nice Girls often are targets for con artists, rapists, and other attackers. Because Nice Girls tend to be focused outside of themselves—helping others, worrying about not hurting others' feelings—they don't focus enough attention on protecting themselves, their feelings, and their very safety. In Karen's case, she was so busy being nice that she didn't pay attention to her instincts and did not check out how others felt about the man. She was so concerned about her image—another common Nice Girl trait—that she didn't report a man who was dangerous to other women.

Because Nice Girls tend to be gullible and to give others the benefit of the doubt, they are far more likely to be taken advantage of, cheated on, abused, or abandoned by their partners than are not-so-nice girls. Cindy suspected for quite some time that her husband was having an affair. He started having to work late and was no longer interested in having sex with her, and she even thought she smelled perfume on his shirts when he came home. But each time she confronted him, he swore to her that it was not true. He seemed so sincere and so deeply wounded by her accusations that she always doubted herself. "I decided I was just a suspicious person and that it was unfair for me to accuse him when I had no proof," she shared with me during her first session. The reason Cindy had begun seeing me? She found out that her husband was, in fact, having an affair and that it was only one of a series of many.

Nice Girls are also far more likely to be taken for granted, overworked, underpaid, and passed over for promotions than are not-so-nice girls. For example, Kendra was passed over for a promotion two times. Each time, her boss explained that the reason was that he needed her too much where she was. "I just can't function without you," he'd tell her. "You're my right arm." It felt so good to Kendra to be needed that she didn't recognize she was being manipulated. It never occurred to her to ask her boss for a raise since she was so indispensable.

In addition to being targets for abuse and manipulation, there are other reasons to give up your Nice Girl image, namely:

- People don't respect Nice Girls.
- If you don't tell others what makes you angry, upset, unhappy, or disappointed, there is little chance of fixing the problem.
- People don't really know you unless you tell them how you really feel.
- If you don't tell people how you honestly feel, you are being dishonest.
- Unless you are honest about who you are and how you feel, there is little chance of your experiencing true intimacy in your relationships.

Nice Girls Aren't Always Nice

Another reason for giving up your Nice Girl act is that Nice Girls aren't always nice. In fact, they can often be conniving and mean. They often complain about people behind their backs because they are too afraid to confront them to their faces. They can be passive-aggressive—meaning that even though they may be angry at someone, they smile and pretend everything is okay and then do something underhanded to get back at the person. In the past few years, we've been exposed to how girls and women tend to gossip about and backstab one another.

The female gender may be hardwired to be more cooperative and to value connection over confrontation, but these very tendencies often cause girls or women to take their aggression underground. As Rachel Simmons, the author of *Odd Girl Out*, found after interviewing three hundred girls, there is a hidden culture of female aggression. Girls may not be as physically violent as boys are, but there is a silent, often equally destructive form of bullying that occurs between girls. This behavior includes name-calling, snide remarks, dirty looks, gossiping, and starting rumors. Because women value connection so highly, to be excluded from the group may be the ultimate form of revenge or punishment. In some cultures, such as many in the Middle East, women learn a very poignant yet nonviolent way of wielding power with dirty looks, body postures, and silence.

Nice Girls often end relationships without notice when someone better comes along. Nice Girls can be too nice in some areas of their lives and not so nice in others. For example, some Nice Girls put up with unacceptable behavior from their lovers or mates but are impatient, angry, and unreasonable with their children. Some are overly solicitous at work but are rude and demanding at home. Often, Nice Girls put up with unacceptable behavior for so long that they finally blow. Then they feel horribly guilty, apologize profusely, and overcompensate by being super nice to the person in the future.

The Seven Types of Nice Girls

Every woman has some Nice Girl in her, but some have more than others. For this reason, this book will be of particular interest to the following types of women:

1. The Doormat. This is the stereotypical passive female who allows others to walk all over her. She suffers from "terminal niceness" and never seems to learn her lesson no matter how many times she is taken advantage of, manipulated, betrayed,

or abused. Women with Doormat syndrome are often the victims of unscrupulous salespeople and con artists. Many are also emotionally, verbally, or physically abused, and they tend to take the abuse for months and even years.

2. The Pretender. This type of woman has a powerful investment in appearing to be nice, cooperative, and charming (when in reality she may be angry and resentful). She pretends she agrees when she actually doesn't. And she often pretends to be interested in what others are saying or doing while in reality she is bored.

3. The Innocent. This type of Nice Girl is very naive and gullible. She is quick to believe what others tell her and is therefore easily manipulated or conned. An Innocent often continues to defend partners or children who are selfish, deceitful, or blatantly abusive, even when everyone around her tries to tell her she is being used or abused.

4. The Victim. This type of woman feels hopeless and helpless to change her circumstances in life. In her attempts to be nice she has repressed her power to such an extent that she has lost touch with it completely. Those who suffer from this type of Nice Girl syndrome have been known to stay with a physically abusive man even after being hospitalized several times.

5. The Martyr. This type of woman sacrifices herself for others—her parents, her partner, and/or her children. This includes sacrificing her time, her own financial security, even her health in order to help or rescue others. Often the martyr will devote her life to helping others, and then she will feel that these people owe her because of her sacrifices.

6. The Prude. The prude has a strong need to be perfect or moral. She adheres to rigid standards (for example, no sex before marriage, no alcohol) and is often active in a conservative religious church. She strongly disapproves of certain behaviors and is very judgmental of others who engage in activities she disapproves of. But she hides her disapproval behind a wall of niceness.

7. The Enlightened One. This type of woman believes strongly in tolerance, compassion, and forgiveness to such an extent

that she represses her anger and doesn't allow herself to express such normal feelings as sadness, envy, anger, or resentment.

Anita and Donna: A Martyr and an Innocent

Anita hadn't been happy with her husband, Edward, for a long time. Over the years, he had grown distant. He seldom talked to her about anything of import and was rarely affectionate toward her. Their life together seemed empty and boring. She begged him to go to counseling, but he refused.

Whenever Anita thought about leaving Edward, she would remind herself that he had some good qualities and, after all, he was sweet and generous with their two children. "I wanted to end our marriage, but I just couldn't bear to hurt him. I thought it would devastate him if he ever lost me and if he couldn't see the kids every day. I imagined him in some dark apartment just fading away."

So Anita stayed with Edward month after empty month, year after boring year. She became deeply depressed and began taking a prescription drug to lift her moods. Then one day she got a phone call. It was a woman begging Anita to let Edward go. "She told me she and Edward had been in love for a long time and that he'd been promising to leave me for years, but he couldn't abandon me. I was absolutely shocked. All those years wasted. All those years when I could have been happy with someone else, and here *he* was the one with someone else! I felt like such an idiot."

Anita is a good example of a martyr. Like many women, she sacrificed her own happiness for that of someone else. She felt it would be selfish to think of her own needs first. She couldn't tolerate the idea of being responsible for someone else's unhappiness. Like many women, Anita believed strongly in being fair. She always tried to balance out any critical feelings she had of someone (in this case, her distant husband) by trying to also see the person's good points.

Donna's husband is emotionally and sometimes physically abusive toward her. "He doesn't beat me or anything like that. He just pushes me around a little. And he's always sorry afterward," Donna explained. When I told Donna that her husband's abusive behavior would likely escalate, she said, "Oh, no. He's not a batterer or anything. He's just under a lot of pressure right now at work and, frankly, I think I sometimes provoke him. I need to learn to keep my big mouth shut."

Donna is what I call an Innocent. Women like Donna jeopardize their happiness, their safety, and sometimes their very lives because they are naive. Their gullibility blinds them to the manipulations and harmful behaviors of others. They want to believe that other people are good no matter how much evidence there is to the contrary.

Why do so many women like Anita and Donna think and behave in these ways? In this book, you will find the answers to that question, as well as to the following:

- Why can't many women bear to hurt another person, even when holding back means hurting themselves?

- How does the need to give others the benefit of the doubt make some women blind, deaf, and dumb when it comes to spotting unhealthy behaviors in their spouses, children, and others?

- Why do some women prefer to see only the good side of others?

- Why do some women always blame themselves?

- Why is it that so many women have difficulty confronting those who hurt or anger them?

- Why is it, in these enlightened times, that women continue to sacrifice themselves for their mates, their friends, and their bosses?

- Why is it that females who are abused as children often end up being revictimized as adults, whereas males who are abused as children often end up becoming victimizers?

- How do women, in some ways, play a role in their own victimization?

You'll learn the myriad ways that being nice prevents you from achieving the success and happiness that is rightfully yours. *The Nice Girl Syndrome* will show you how girls and women are socialized to be nice and how this socialization sets them up for failure, unhappiness, and even abuse. Most important, it will show you how to transform yourself from a Nice Girl to a Strong Woman.

Nice Girls versus Strong Women

Strong Women are not girls at all. The word *girl* is supposed to be used to describe young females—not grown women. Yet the word *girls* is often used to describe even mature women. This may serve to make women feel younger, but it also takes away their power. For this reason, apart from our term "Nice Girls," we will use the word *woman* exclusively when talking about any female over the age of eighteen.

So how do we differentiate a Strong Woman from a Nice Girl?

- Strong Women have learned that niceness does not guarantee that others will treat them fairly or with respect. They know that by being too nice, they actually encourage others to walk all over them. They've learned they have to earn respect by first respecting themselves and then by demanding the respect of others.

- Strong Women never put their safety or their self-esteem aside to please someone else or to keep a man. If someone acts inappropriately or abusively in any way (including becoming emotionally abusive), Strong Women stand up for themselves and make it abundantly clear that they will not tolerate the abuse. If this doesn't work, they walk away.

- Strong Women want men in their lives but not at the price of their safety, their children's safety, their self-respect, their self-esteem, or their peace of mind.

- Strong Women know what they want and believe they have a right to have it and can figure out by themselves how to go after it. They don't walk over anyone along the way, but they don't let anyone walk over them, either.

- Strong Women respect the rights of others, but if their own rights are not honored and respected, they know how to stand up for themselves.

- Strong Women realize their voices have power, so instead of remaining silent to avoid displeasing someone or hurting someone's feelings, they let people know where they stand on important issues. They understand it is far more important to be true to themselves and their beliefs than for someone to like them.

- Strong Women work toward making themselves the best version of themselves they can become and then expect others, especially men, to accept and appreciate them the way they are. They aren't willing to change just to please someone else, and they have the wisdom to realize that if someone doesn't accept them there is always another who will.

- Strong Women have learned that a lot of feminine behavior and attitudes simply no longer work (for example, that women need men to support and protect them). They've had the courage to discard these outdated beliefs and ways of acting and to embrace an entirely different way of life. For example, in the past being nice could get a woman pretty far. If she was a Nice Girl, people looked upon her fondly and went out of their way to treat her well. If she was a Nice Girl, she gained a good reputation in her community. Boys treated her with respect and protected her from danger—including from the lurking eyes and lurching hands of those unscrupulous types who would dare to take advantage of a Nice Girl. If she was nice enough and pretty enough, she would probably get herself a man.

  Today, all that has changed. Being nice no longer guarantees that you will be treated with kindness and respect. Having a good reputation can't protect you from the tremendous backlash that is occurring against women. While books like *The Rules* still teach women that they need to be nice to capture a man, the men Nice Girls capture are usually not worth having.

- Strong Women have learned that they can't depend on others to save or protect them. They've learned that few chivalrous heroes or supermen exist to pluck them from the arms of danger. Consider the occurrence several years ago in New York City's Central Park after the Puerto Rican Day parade. Many women were harassed, taunted, and even attacked while bystanders of both genders stood by and did nothing to protect them. By many accounts, the police refused to help, even when women specifically asked them to intervene. With the exception of one man who quietly led a woman to safety, other men either stood idly by while women were being molested, or they joined in the melee. Because of this lack of support from others, Strong Women have learned they have to save and protect themselves—physically and emotionally. They have become their own heroes.

- Strong Women have learned that being too nice can have dire consequences, that there can be no room in their lives for being naive and innocent. It simply isn't safe, since it invites others to take advantage of them. And it isn't honorable, since it is often used as an excuse for women to avoid taking responsibility for themselves.

How Do Nice Girls Become Strong Women?

Being too nice can be a difficult habit to break. Because this unhealthy behavior is instilled in women at a very early age, some women have an easier time shedding it than others do. Letting go of the need to be seen as fair, understanding, or even selfless can be a painful process. Some have a fear of confrontation, most often brought about from having experienced constant conflict in their childhood homes or having been emotionally or physically abused as children. More than simply becoming more assertive or learning to establish boundaries, the process of letting go of niceness involves unearthing and then discarding deeply buried false beliefs and replacing them with the truth.

In this book, you will get help in unearthing these often illusive false beliefs. You will then learn to replace these unhealthy and false beliefs with healthy ways of thinking about yourself and others.

So how do Nice Girls become Strong Women? By confronting the beliefs, attitudes, and behaviors that keep you stuck in your Nice Girl act and by replacing these beliefs, attitudes, and behaviors with others that will empower you.

I'll start out by encouraging you to examine your beliefs and attitudes. Once you have come to recognize how they contribute to your unhappiness and to negative patterns, you will need to take action. Some of the action steps you will be encouraged to take include the following:

- Stop playing sweet, gullible, and naive. It's outdated and it invites people, especially men, to take advantage of you.

- Stop giving people second (and third and fourth) chances. If someone shows you who he or she is, pay attention and act accordingly.

- Stop being fair and start being strong. Women's need for fairness often gets them into trouble. Their tendency to want to look at both sides of a situation often blurs the real issue and allows them to be easily manipulated.

- Learn that setting limits and boundaries and expecting others to take care of their own needs can be the greatest act of kindness you can perform. You don't do anyone a favor by allowing people to take advantage of you.

- Let others know when they have hurt or angered you. By not speaking up when someone insults or mistreats you, you are inadvertently giving permission for him or her to continue to treat you in the same way in the future.

- Confront your own anger. Sometimes under all that niceness lies a huge storage bin of repressed and suppressed anger.

- Acknowledge that often the real reason you take care of others is because you secretly want to be taken care of. You hope the person you've been taking care of will turn around and take care of you in the same way.

- Acknowledge that sometimes it is easier to sacrifice yourself for others than to focus on your own problems or take the risk of going after your own goals.

- Be honest with yourself about your real reasons for being a Nice Girl. When we look for the motive for our niceness, we often find guilt, shame, fear of confrontation, fear of rejection, and an intense fear of being alone.

- Allow yourself to be bad sometimes. It's not only okay to be bad but it is healthy. In fact, if you don't allow yourself to be bad at times, you will continue to attract people into your life who will act out your badness for you.

Melanie is always attracted to bad boys. This is how she explained it: "I like them because they're so sexy, and they're so much fun. Nice guys are boring." But Melanie gets hurt a lot, too. Many of her bad-boy boyfriends have cheated on her, and some have become physically abusive.

Melanie is not alone. Many women, even though it is against their better judgment, are attracted to bad boys. This is especially true of Nice Girls. Nice Girls like bad boys because they do all the things Nice Girls wish they could do but can't. It isn't a coincidence that girls who are raised by strict parents or in deeply religious families are often the ones who get involved with bad boys. It's their way of rebelling against all the rules; they're being bad vicariously, without having to take responsibility for it.

The Four C's

In a no-holds-barred manner, *The Nice Girl Syndrome* will challenge you to confront those beliefs, attitudes, and behaviors that invite others to take advantage of, manipulate, and abuse you, and will show you how to give up your "sweetness and light" image once and for all and replace it with an image made up of what I call the four power C's: confidence, competence, conviction, and courage.

- *Confidence.* The reason many women are too nice is that they lack the confidence to stand up for themselves, say no, disagree, or state their preferences. They fall back on the old standby niceness to get by because they do not believe in themselves or that other people will respect their wishes, preferences, or ideas. In this book, I will teach you how to gain the kind of confidence you need to become a Strong Woman.

- *Competence.* Most women are more competent than they realize. But because they have been taught to be modest and even self-deprecating, they believe that acting competent is the same as acting conceited, cocky, or narcissistic. I will teach you the differences between acting competent and acting conceited and help you to become more comfortable in the role of a Strong, Competent Woman.

- *Conviction.* Many women were taught that they should never disagree or argue with others, especially authority figures. Others become intimidated by those who are domineering or overly confident. Still others believe that they should avoid conflict at all costs. In this book, I will help you to risk standing up for your convictions, even if it means upsetting someone else or creating conflict.

- *Courage*. It takes courage to become more confident and to then show it to others. It takes courage to own your competence and to stop hiding it from others. And it especially takes courage to stand by your convictions. In this book, I will help you to tap into your inherent courage—the courage you were born with—and to strengthen your courage by taking small risks in the beginning and building on them.

These four power C's will arm you with everything you need to make the transformation from Nice Girl to Strong Woman.

2

How Did We Get So Nice?

The first problem for all of us, men and women, is
not to learn, but to unlearn.
—GLORIA STEINEM

What are the causes of the Nice Girl syndrome? There are
many causes, some of which we will discuss in this chapter
and all of which will be discussed in the book.

The Four Causes of Nice Girl Syndrome

Generally speaking, there are four major origins for Nice Girl
behavior:

- *Biological* predisposition
- *Societal* beliefs passed on to a child by the culture or society in
  which she is raised
- *Familial* beliefs passed on to a child by her family, either
  directly or by witnessing parental and other family members'
  behavior
- *Experiential* beliefs a child forms as a result of her personal
  experiences, including childhood trauma

Biological Predisposition

Women are hard-wired to be patient and compassionate and to value
connection over confrontation. Professor Carol Gilligan, in her
landmark studies at Harvard University, came to the conclusion that

what has previously been considered "female passivity" is often a woman's need to seek a solution that is most inclusive of everyone's needs, "as an act of care rather than the restraint of aggression."

Most recently, a landmark UCLA study suggests that women actually have a larger behavioral repertoire than the "fight or flight" choices to which men appear to be limited. When the hormone oxytocin is released as part of the stress response in a woman, it buffers the fight-or-flight response and encourages her to tend to children and gather with other women.

Societal Beliefs

Girls are typically socialized to be polite, appropriate, pleasant, and agreeable—all the personality traits that characterize Nice Girls. For centuries, being nice was often synonymous with being female. Girls were supposed to be "sugar and spice and everything nice." Unfortunately, even today, the feminine ideal tends to be to please others; be selfless, nice, and pretty; and make oneself the object of someone else's life.

To attain this culturally prescribed ideal, a teenage girl must put away a great many parts of herself. She stops speaking out and expressing her feelings. Instead, she focuses on trying to please others, especially those of the opposite sex.

Familial Beliefs

Your family passed down to you certain messages and beliefs. These include everything from the way people should treat one another to the role women play in a family. These messages and beliefs have a powerful influence on your thinking and behavior and help shape who you are today.

For example, Janine was raised in a home where girls and women were viewed as second-class citizens. Her father was considered to be the head of the household and made all the decisions. Janine's mother never contradicted him. Janine and her sisters were expected to serve her father and brothers the best cuts of meat and to save plenty of food for them in case they wanted seconds. Janine had to ask her father's permission before she and her mother could buy her school clothes or books, and she had to get his okay before she went out with her friends, even if it was just to play in the backyard.

What did Janine learn from her parents' messages and beliefs?

She learned that merely by having been born female she was inferior to men. She learned to be passive and to not trust her own judgment. She also learned that it was okay for a man to dominate her. She ended up marrying just such a man. Today, Janine has to ask her husband's permission before she goes out with her female friends from work. She has to ask his permission to spend money. Janine learned to be a victim from both her father and her mother.

There are several common types of family situations that can set a woman up to be a Nice Girl. These include:

- Having a passive mother
- Having an abusive or tyrannical father or older brother
- Being raised in an ultra-conservative or deeply religious family in which women are considered to be second-class citizens
- Being raised in a misogynistic family
- Having parents who place a high value on women's being fair, compassionate, and nice

The first false belief, that other people's feelings and needs are more important than one's own, usually comes from being taught this at home. This belief may have been modeled by a passive or codependent mother who sacrificed herself for her family or her husband, never considering that she had needs of her own. A girl growing up with such a mother can easily receive the message that to be a good woman, a good wife, or a good mother, she must put her own needs aside and focus solely on the needs of others.

Another way that a woman may have received this message is if she had a selfish or narcissistic parent who considered his or her needs to be all-important and who ignored the needs of his or her child. A girl raised in this environment often comes to believe that her happiness lies in fulfilling the needs of others.

Experiential Beliefs

It is quite common for Nice Girls to have experienced physical, emotional, or sexual abuse in their childhood or as adults. Abuse and neglect can create certain unhealthy attitudes and beliefs that set women up to be Nice Girls and often victims. For example, those who end up becoming a Nice Girl or taking on a victim stance tend to:

- Blame themselves when something goes wrong

- Believe their needs are not as important as those of others
- Doubt themselves, including doubting their perceptions, their knowledge, and their beliefs
- Be overly trusting of others, even when someone has proven to be untrustworthy
- Be naive when it comes to the motives of others
- Believe they should attempt to meet the needs of others (especially those of their partner and children) no matter the consequences or hardships to themselves and that their own needs are not as important as those of others

In addition to these four major sources of the Nice Girl syndrome, there are other causes as well. Here are the top ten reasons women tend to be too nice:

1. They are afraid that unless they are nice, others will not like them.
2. They are afraid that if they aren't nice, others won't be nice to them.
3. They are afraid of confrontation and conflict.
4. They are afraid of being rejected or abandoned by those they love.
5. They are afraid of being ostracized from their social circle of other women.
6. They are afraid of their anger, of what they might do if they get in touch with it.
7. They are afraid of becoming like an abusive parent.
8. They are afraid of being seen as too masculine.
9. They are afraid of being called a "bitch" or a "ball-breaker."
10. They are afraid that if they aren't nice, men will not protect them and provide for them.

The Fear Factor

As we can see, fear is the predominant factor here. Why are women so fearful? There are multitude reasons, many of which center around the mere fact that as females we are the "weaker" sex, at least physically. The truth is that most men *are* bigger and stronger than most women and, for this very reason, women are often intimidated by men. We aren't necessarily conscious of this on an everyday basis, but the fear is there, nevertheless. It is similar to how a small dog feels next to a large dog. The two dogs can coexist and even play and romp with each other, but make no mistake about it—the smaller dog knows her limits. She knows that if the larger dog wanted to, he could overpower her.

The other factor, closely related to the size differential, is that men carry a built-in weapon they can use against women—their penis. Most men don't think of their penis as a weapon, and most women don't, either. But even so, an erect penis can be used to penetrate, harm, and dominate a woman. Again, it isn't that women consciously think of this on a day-to-day basis, but the inherent fear is there on an unconscious level.

These two physical factors influence a woman's thinking and feeling. We know that our very safety is dependent on the goodwill of men. If we cross them, if we make them angry, we risk being physically reprimanded. Although most men do not use their physical advantage against women, the possibility and the threat are ever present.

The other reason for women's inherent fear is our history of being dominated by men. Throughout the ages, physical force has been used by more dominant groups in society to keep subordinate populations in their place. Men have always been physically larger and stronger than most women, and most societies have been male dominated. Because of this, for centuries, women have been frequent victims of physical assault and intimidation by men and have, in response, been afraid of men.

In ancient Roman times, a man was allowed by law to chastise, divorce, or even kill his wife for adultery or just for attending public games. During the Middle Ages, a man's right to beat his wife was beyond question, yet a woman could be burned alive for so much as threatening her husband.

It took centuries before any real efforts were made to curtail the situation. Few people viewed violence in the home as a problem. The common notion—in Britain and the United States in the past and in many societies today, such as India and Africa—was that a woman is not a full human being but considered property, first of her father, then of her husband.

The third reason girls and women are so afraid is the fact that we continue to be dominated and abused by men. Although much has been done to alleviate domestic violence and the sexual abuse of children, the fact is that these two crimes are still rampant in every culture around the world. Women are still being physically and emotionally abused by their husbands in record numbers, and the rate of childhood sexual abuse continues to climb. Once a girl or a woman has been abused, either emotionally, physically, or sexually, she is overwhelmed by fear and shame. In fact, for many women, their very lives are characterized by the fear that they will once again be victimized. Although this isn't usually done on a conscious level, what better way to keep a female child down than to sexually molest her? As we have learned, rape and sexual abuse are usually more about power and control than about sexuality.

These fears are at the core of most, if not all, of the false beliefs that cause the Nice Girl syndrome. For this reason, I will remind you periodically of the origins of these fears. I will do this to take away some of the shame many women feel because of their passive behavior. For example, many women are unable to leave abusive relationships, even though they know they should. But the reason they stay isn't because they are weak or stupid or because they are masochists who want to be mistreated. It is because they are afraid, and they are afraid for all the reasons I have written about here.

If you are a woman who is often perplexed by her Nice Girl behavior, reminding yourself of the fears that trigger such responses will help you to understand yourself better, not be so critical of yourself, and, hopefully, feel more motivated to change.

3

The Ten False Beliefs That Set Women Up to Be Used and Abused

Man [woman] is made by his [her] belief.
As he [she] believes, so he [she] is.

—BHAGAVAD GITA

To make the transformation from Nice Girl to Strong Woman, you need to unearth and then discard the deeply buried false beliefs that are responsible for your Nice Girl behavior. In this chapter, we will focus on the first part of this equation—unearthing the false beliefs that lie underneath your Nice Girl attitudes and acts. Following are the ten most damaging beliefs that can create the Nice Girl syndrome, along with an explanation as to why and how each belief contributes to Nice Girl behavior.

The Ten False Beliefs

Even though there are different types of Nice Girls, they often have certain beliefs and attitudes in common. These are:

1. Other people's feelings and needs are far more important than my own.

2. If I am nice (and fair) to other people, they will be nice (and fair) to me.

3. What other people think about me is more important than my self-esteem, my health, or even my safety.

33

4. If I am good and perfect, I will be accepted and loved.

5. If I act naive and innocent, people will take care of me and I won't have to grow up.

6. I don't have the right to stand up for myself or act on my own behalf.

7. Anger is a destructive emotion and shouldn't be expressed, especially directly to those with whom you are angry.

8. It is better to avoid conflict at all costs.

9. There is good in everyone, and if you give someone enough chances, he or she will eventually show it to you.

10. Women need men to protect them and support them financially.

I suggest you go back up to the top of this list and circle the sentences that you believe are true. For some of you, this may mean that you actually circle each one of these beliefs, whereas others may circle only one or two. Now put a checkmark next to those beliefs that you still act on even though you really don't believe they are true.

These circled and checkmarked items will be the false beliefs you will need to exorcise out of your mind and heart. In addition to the information in this chapter, there will be a separate chapter devoted to each of these false beliefs in part 2 of the book.

As you read over the list, you may notice that there may be a seed of truth that mutated into some of these false beliefs. For example, although there certainly is good in everyone, we don't have to get burned over and over again by waiting around for it to finally emerge in someone. Kindness and tolerance can often soften even the hardest heart, but these traits can also be an open invitation for others to continue manipulating and taking advantage of us.

Nice Girls need to learn that these beliefs and attitudes are simply not working for them. In some cases, this is due to the fact that Nice Girls need to practice beliefs and attitudes opposite to those listed. For example, it is true that anger can be a destructive emotion; many people cause a great deal of harm to others because their anger is out of control. But this is generally not true of Nice Girls, who tend to have the opposite problem—that of repressing and suppressing their anger. They usually need to give themselves permission to acknowledge, feel, and express their anger in constructive ways, to not continue to ignore or deny righteous anger. They need to learn that anger itself is not a negative or destructive emotion—it is what we choose to do with it that determines whether it is positive or negative.

In many cases, women have been brainwashed to believe these false beliefs, often starting when they were small children. Sometimes this brainwashing came from society at large; other times, it came from specific messages or behavior from parents or other authority figures.

How Do We Reverse This Brainwashing?

Needless to say, it can sometimes be difficult to reverse this brainwashing and help women to face the truth. In part 2, I offer remedies specifically designed to counter false beliefs and to help install beliefs that are more conducive to becoming a Strong Woman. I also offer the concept of "positive and powerful statements" to help counter the negative messages that drive Nice Girl behavior.

Positive and powerful statements are sentences that you will create to help cancel out the false beliefs that have contributed to, or in some cases, created, your Nice Girl behavior. Until very recently, it was accepted that early childhood was the only time when the brain was malleable enough to be significantly influenced by external stimuli. However, in the last decade or so, new technology has revealed that even adult brains are changing in response to stimuli. Most important, we now know that brains can be significantly restructured under the right learning conditions.

This is where positive and powerful statements come in. The more you repeat a positive and powerful statement, the stronger the neural pathway becomes and the greater your ability to "rewire" your brain. Generally speaking, a positive and powerful statement is the *opposite* of a false belief. For example, let's take the first false belief, "Other people's feelings and needs are far more important than my own." What would be the opposite of that statement? It would probably be something like, "My feelings and needs are as important as anyone else's," or even (God forbid a Nice Girl would say this), "My feelings and needs are more important than anyone else's."

As you read each of the chapters in part 2, I will recommend that you create a positive and powerful statement to counter each false belief and that you repeat that new belief to yourself over and over, several times a day. Retraining requires repetition. This repetition, along with the remedies suggested at the end of each chapter, will help you alleviate these false beliefs from your life.

Are positive and powerful statements like affirmations? No. Affirmations usually don't stick because there isn't the strong limbic component. Affirmations are more a cognitive exercise, whereas positive and powerful statements are focused, intensive work aimed at retraining the brain.

Let's examine each false belief more closely to help you recognize exactly why it is a false belief, recognize how each false belief contributes to the Nice Girl syndrome, and help you begin to recognize where this false belief comes from in you.

False Belief #1: Other People's Feelings and Needs Are Far More Important than My Own

It is extremely difficult to prove to most women that this is actually a false belief. "What do you mean?" you might be thinking. "Of course we need to think of others first. Otherwise, we are just being selfish."

One of the main reasons women believe that thinking of their own needs first is selfish is that biologically those of the female gender of any species are hardwired to be mothers and nurturers. Until very recently, girls and women were considered to be the caretakers of the family. (Nature has an investment in mothers' being unselfish when it comes to their children—otherwise, their young would be left to their own devices and would starve or go unprotected and be killed.)

You may think that every human being is taught to put others' feelings and needs first when he or she is young, because adults wish to teach all children to be kind, considerate, and generous, but this simply isn't true. It seems that girls are taught it much more than boys.

Girls are repeatedly taught that they should put the needs of others before their own and that they are selfish if they think of their own needs first. Although some boys are taught this belief as well, they are not generally taught to consider other people's feelings at the expense of their own, as girls are taught.

Rachel Simmons, the author of the best-selling book *Odd Girl Out: The Hidden Culture of Aggression in Girls*, found that this need to put other people's feelings first was a theme that ran through her interviews with girls. No matter how upset they were, the girls said that they would rather not hurt someone else's feelings. Their own needs seemed utterly expendable. They learned to shrink their problems and feelings into "little things," calling them "unimportant," "stupid," and "not worth a fight," and to stow them away somewhere inside.

For many girls, the message of putting others ahead of themselves is conveyed more by the examples of their mothers than by actual words. It is a powerful message, nevertheless. Girls who watch their mothers sacrifice their own needs and desires for those of their husbands on a daily basis receive the message loud and clear that their fathers' needs are more important than their mothers'.

In some homes, particularly where there is rampant misogyny, girls are taught that the feelings and needs of males are more important than those of females. They are forced to wait on the male members of the family and allow the boys and men (including even younger brothers) to tell them what to do. The definition of *misogyny* is "a distrust, fear, dislike, or hatred of females." Inherent in misogynistic beliefs is that males are superior to females. As antiquated as misogyny may seem to be, it is a powerful force in many cultures and religions today—both in the United States and in the rest of the world.

In other families, particularly those where parents are self-absorbed or even narcissistic, the message is: *My* needs are more important than yours, or anyone else's, for that matter. Self-absorbed and narcissistic parents teach their child that his or her own needs do not matter. Instead of meeting their child's needs, these parents expect him or her to cater to and take care of them. In some cases, there is a reversal of roles: the child becomes the parent and vice versa. A child in this kind of family situation is often referred to as "parentified." Such a child functions the way a parent should, making sure that the parent's emotional and sometimes physical needs are met. We will discuss this phenomenon in much more depth in part 2.

Sherry: "I'd Rather Be the One Who Is Hurt"

Another version of the false belief "Other people's feelings and needs are far more important than my own" is the belief "I'd rather be the one who is hurt than to hurt someone else." Although many of my Nice Girl clients have acted on this belief, no one actually verbalized it to me until I began working with Sherry. During one of our sessions, much to my surprise, Sherry uttered these words: "It hurts me too much to disappoint or hurt someone else. I feel so guilty. I'd rather be the one who is hurt. I can take that. But I can't take knowing that I was the one to hurt someone else."

When Sherry was growing up, her mother always made her feel horribly guilty when she focused on her own needs or tried to stand up for herself. "How can you do this to me? You know I need you so much, you're the only one who is there for me," her mother would say. Sherry's mother and father fought constantly, and her mother used her as a confidante, telling her private information about her father and their relationship—information she should not have been privy to.

False Belief #2: If I Am Nice (and Fair) to Other People, They Will Be Nice (and Fair) to Me

At the core of this belief is the assumption that by being nice, you can avoid painful experiences such as someone getting angry with you, disapproving of you, or rejecting or abandoning you.

But this belief borders on superstition—and is just as effective. You might as well throw salt over your shoulder to ward off evil spirits as to believe that being nice to other people will guarantee that they will be nice to you.

On the surface, this belief makes sense. It only stands to reason that by doing unto others as we would have them do unto us, we will elicit positive responses from them. Generally speaking, this is what happens. But there are four major flaws to this belief:

1. Just because you are nice to people doesn't guarantee they will be nice to you, since everyone has his or her own issues. There are people who will not be nice to you (or like you) no matter how nice you are to them. This may be because they are prejudiced against you (you are a woman, you have a dark complexion, you are "too fat" or "too thin" or "too short"), because they are envious of you, or because you remind them of someone else whom they dislike. There are many reasons that people may not return your niceness and that often have nothing to do with how you act or who you are.

2. There are people who can and will cause you harm even if you are nice. Some people are, by their very nature, short tempered, impatient, demanding, controlling, or abusive.

3. Sometimes Nice Girls are so nice that it turns people off. This may be because they sense that your niceness is not genuine, or because your niceness seems to have a price tag on it. Or it may be that they don't respect you because you are so nice. Nice Girls are often viewed as being too compliant or too ingratiating, and this can turn some people off.

4. There are people in the world who will take advantage of your niceness or who interpret niceness as an open invitation to be cruel.

Bad things do, indeed, happen to good people. Nice Girls get hurt, rejected, and disliked by others all the time. Not because of what they have done but just because.

Closely related to the belief that being nice to others will guarantee that others will be nice to you is the belief that if you are fair to others, they will be fair toward you. But once again, this is often not the case. You can be fair toward someone and have that person turn around and be unfair toward you—often for the same reasons as I listed above.

False Belief #3: What Other People Think about Me Is More Important than My Self-Esteem, My Health, or Even My Safety

Like many false beliefs, this one is not something that women consciously think about and decide to believe. If you were to ask them, most women might even say that they don't really believe this. But unfortunately, their behavior belies such a declaration. They show by their actions, especially their behavior with men, that what others think of them is indeed more important than nearly anything else in their lives.

Women repeatedly starve themselves because they want to be accepted by others. They put their health at risk because they care so much about what other people think. In fact, the crisis surrounding women and their body image has to do with women's belief that others judge them solely on their appearance. They are willing to sacrifice almost anything for the acceptance and approval of others.

As was discovered from research by Carol Gilligan, a pioneer in the study of women's development, in her book *In a Different Voice: Psychological Theory and Women's Development*, relationships play an unusually important role in girls' social development. Girls and women care deeply about what others think about them. In fact, much of their self-esteem centers around whether others perceive them in a positive or a negative light, and for this reason they have been known to do embarrassing, hurtful, even dangerous things to garner the approval of others.

Nice Girls frequently go along with the crowd, whether it is drinking alcohol or taking drugs; agreeing to activities, including sexual ones, that they really don't want to do; or even breaking the law to gain or keep the approval of a man or of a group.

My client Jennifer was referred to me by her mother, who discovered that Jennifer had been engaging in group sex with girls and boys from school. This behavior had been going on for some time and would have continued except that the mother had been contacted by the Public Health Department when it was discovered that Jennifer, along with several others in the group, had contracted syphilis.

At first, Jennifer refused to talk about her experiences, but gradually she opened up to me. Although she had a few close friends in high school, she always longed to fit in with the popular kids. "I just wasn't in their league," she shared with me. "My parents don't have the money theirs do, and I can't buy the kind of clothes they wear. They seemed to have so much fun; they were always laughing and kidding around with each other. I wanted to have fun like that."

Then Jason, one of the popular boys, suddenly began to take an interest in Jennifer, and she was thrilled. He was great-looking and popular, and he came from a wealthy family. Even though he was only a sophomore, he drove a brand new Lexus. When he asked Jennifer to join him and his friends after school, she gladly agreed.

They went to the home of one of his friends. There were no parents around and the kids helped themselves to the liquor cabinet and the beer in the refrigerator. Before Jennifer knew it, she was feeling no pain. Jason began to kiss her while they sat on the couch, and Jennifer felt as if she was in heaven. She was being kissed by one of the most popular guys at school! She couldn't wait to tell her friends.

But when Jason put his hand down Jennifer's blouse, she pushed him away. She felt he was going too fast; besides, there were other people around. When she explained this to Jason, he just smiled and pulled her into a nearby bedroom. She didn't resist. Within minutes, Jason was penetrating her. Jennifer's head was spinning, and she didn't know what to do. She'd had sex before but never so quickly with a boy she didn't know. However, she really liked Jason and wanted him to like her back.

Afterward, Jennifer felt a little embarrassed, but Jason reassured her that she was hot and that he really liked her. He was very polite and took her home. She hoped he would call her again.

The next day at school, Jason was cordial but certainly not friendly. When Jennifer went over to his table in the cafeteria he acted as if nothing had happened between them. Jennifer felt humiliated and used as she slunk back to her table.

Much to Jennifer's surprise, about a week later, Jason came by her table and asked her if she'd like to join him and his friends for a party after school. Jennifer jumped at the chance.

This time, they went to the house of another of Jason's friends, again with no parents around. They all started drinking, and several couples started making out on the couches. Jason pulled Jennifer down on one of the couches next to another couple and started kissing and fondling her. Jennifer felt really embarrassed to be acting like this in front of others, but when she tried to pull away, Jason said, "I should never have asked you here. You're just too square." This hurt her feelings. She looked around and noticed that several of the kids were having sex, right there in the living room. She so desperately wanted to be part of the group. If they could act like this and not be embarrassed, why couldn't she? And so she allowed Jason to take off her blouse and touch and kiss her breasts. Then she allowed him to have sex with her. Once, when she opened her eyes, she noticed that other people were watching them.

This was to be the beginning of a downward slope for Jennifer. She went from having sex with Jason in front of the other kids to allowing Jason's friends to have sex with her. Although she felt a lot of shame about her behavior, she feared that if she said no she would be kicked out of the group. At school she had became one of the popular girls, and she simply wasn't willing to let that go, no matter what she had to do. It just felt too good to be treated like she was so special, to feel the envy of the other kids, some of whom had been her friends in the past.

The group eventually moved on from swapping partners to having group sex. This was the most degrading part of all. Jennifer felt she was a piece of meat to be passed around from boy to boy. Sometimes two boys would have sex with her at the same time, and other times they'd line up to have sex with her. One day she had sex with ten boys.

Although Jennifer always drank each time they partied, she never got so drunk that she erased the images from her mind. By the time she came into therapy, her self-esteem was at an all-time low. "I keep seeing these scenes in my mind—like something out of a pornographic movie. But instead of some slut being gang-raped by a group of men, it is me in the picture."

In spite of the fact that she had contracted a sexually transmitted disease and had been humiliated when her parents found out what she had done, Jennifer was still having a difficult time giving up her association with the popular kids. "Do you know what it would be like for me if I wasn't part of that group anymore? I'd have to go back to my old table with my tail between my legs. I wouldn't get all the special privileges I get from being part of the popular group. People will look at me entirely differently."

Jennifer was still willing to put her dignity aside and to continue damaging her self-esteem just to be popular. Even more concerning, she was still willing to endanger her health.

Jennifer's case may seem like an extreme example to you, but think about this a moment: What have you done in your life to get or keep the approval of others? Have you gone along with the crowd, even when your instincts told you that what they were doing was unhealthy, perhaps even dangerous? This might include taking drugs because everyone else was doing it, driving too fast because your friends told you to go faster, or sleeping with a guy because you thought he would dump you if you didn't. How many times have you put your own best interests aside to gain the acceptance of a group or individual, to be part of the group, or to look good to your group or to the public?

In *Odd Girl Out*, Rachel Simmons calls popularity an "addiction" for girls, "a prize for which some would pay any price." Girls pour boundless energy and anxiety into becoming popular. This quest for popularity can change girls, causing many to lie, cheat, and steal. "They lie to be accepted, cheat their friends by using them, steal people's secrets to resell at a higher social price." One eleven-year-old interviewee told Simmons, "If girls have a chance to be popular, they will take it, and they wouldn't really care who they are hurting."

Mary Pipher, in her best-selling book *Reviving Ophelia: Saving the Selves of Adolescent Girls*, observed that as teenagers, girls desperately want to be accepted. They are faced with an impossible choice: either to remain true to themselves and risk rejection by their friends, or to desert their authentic self and be socially acceptable. Unfortunately, the choice for most girls is obvious: to abandon a large part of themselves so as to gain acceptance.

When Simmons attended a leadership workshop for twenty-five middle-class teenagers (one-third of whom were nonwhite), she discovered some interesting things. When the girls were asked what made them uncomfortable about leadership, nearly every girl voiced a concern that related to how others would react to what they said or did. Over and over, the girls said that looking bad or stupid or "getting judged" was their worst fear. Whether it was meeting new people, speaking in public, reciting, or debating, the girls feared being "shut down." As Simmons explained, "They worried that people would not give them a chance to explain themselves and that others would shatter their self-confidence. As a result, they worried, people would not like them, would not want to be their friends, and [would] turn their backs on them."

False Belief #4: If I Am Good and Perfect, I Will Be Accepted and Loved

For many years, girls were raised to believe that if they were "good," if they minded their parents and did what was expected of them at school, they would in turn be accepted and loved by others. This "sugar and spice and everything nice" mind-set continues into the present in some circles (for example, conservative or deeply religious homes). In these environments, girls are supposed to be sweet and caring, little caregivers in training.

In *Odd Girl Out*, Rachel Simmons cites a 1994 article in *Schoolgirls*, in which journalist Peggy Orenstein wrote: "A good girl is nice before she is anything else—before she is vigorous, bright, even before she is honest." She described the "perfect girl" as: "The girl who has no bad thoughts or feelings, the kind of person everyone wants to be with. . . . [She is] the girl who speaks quietly, calmly, who is always nice and kind, never mean or bossy. . . . She reminds young women to silence themselves rather than speak their true feelings, which they come to consider 'stupid,' 'selfish,' 'rude,' or just plain irrelevant."

After talking to hundreds of girls for her research project on girls and aggression, Simmons found that the girls she interviewed expressed their exasperation at being expected to be nice all the time and to be nice to everyone. One girl expressed her frustration like this: "They expect us to act like girls back in the 1800s!" Another said, "They expect you to be perfect. . . . When boys do bad things, they all know they're going to do bad stuff. When girls do it, they yell at them." Still another said, "They expect you to be perfect angels and then sometimes we don't want to be considered a perfect angel."

Some parents also instill in their children the belief that they have to be perfect. When my mother was alive, she sometimes told me this story: One day, as she dropped me off at the babysitter's and gave me her usual admonishment—"Now you be good for Mrs. Jones today"—I turned to her and said, "I have to be good for Mrs. Jones, I have to be good for you, I have to be good for my teachers, I have to be good at church. When can I be bad?"

My mother always laughed when she told this story, since in many ways she loved my being precocious. But I doubt that she truly appreciated what I was trying to tell her—that I felt too much pressure to be good and perfect.

False Belief #5: If I Act Naive and Innocent, People Will Take Care of Me and I Won't Have to Grow Up

It used to be that the payoff for being sweet and nice was that one was taken care of and protected by the men and authority figures in one's life. Girls and women were perceived as weaker and in need of protection from the "big, bad world" and boys and men took on the responsibility of making sure that nothing bad happened to them. But those days are gone, along with chivalry and manners. Most boys and men today do not feel responsible for protecting girls; in fact, many view girls and women as objects to be exploited. Today, partly due to the popularity of rap music in which girls and women are denigrated and called bitches, boys and men often view girls and women as mere sex objects.

Recently a story on the news related one more case in which several boys raped a girl at a party. As is so often the prelude to such violence, the girl had been drinking too much and had passed out. Instead of the boys' feeling protective of her, they took advantage of the situation. To make matters worse, they videotaped the gang rape and showed it to their friends the next day.

This doesn't mean that there aren't men who like taking on the role of provider and protector. But these men are not necessarily throwbacks to an earlier time—unfortunately, they often take on this role as a way of dominating women. In fact, these men often look for women who are passive, who appear naive and innocent, because such women are easier to control.

Those women who continue to believe that playing sweet, innocent, and naive will guarantee they will be financially provided for by men are also in for a rude awakening. This was the case with my client Maureen, who was raised by a father who instilled in her the belief that women are incapable of taking care of themselves. She grew up hearing her father tease her mother about how inadequate she was, saying that he hoped nothing ever happened to him because he didn't think she could manage without him doing everything for her. Maureen's mother would sweetly laugh and agree with him, seemingly happy with her role as a ditsy wife and mother.

Maureen grew up following in her mother's footsteps. She was attracted to men like her father—take-charge kind of guys who only expected her to look pretty and act sweet. At eighteen she married her Prince Charming, a man who was seven years older than her and already established in his career as a lawyer. Maureen relished her role of homemaker and wife, catering to her husband's every want and need. She knew nothing about their finances, leaving all that "complicated" stuff to her husband, whom she trusted implicitly to look out for her best interests. But Maureen was to pay heavily for her naïveté. After five years of marriage, her husband left her for another woman. Because of his connections in the community with other lawyers, Maureen was unable to find an attorney in town who would represent her in the divorce case. The out-of-town lawyer whom she finally found to take her case told her that she was going to have a huge battle on her hands. Her husband had successfully hidden many of their assets and he was accusing her of being unfaithful to him.

This is what Maureen shared with me during our first session: "I couldn't believe how naive I had been. I simply trusted that he would think of my best interests. That he would always provide for me and protect me from any harm. But *he* was the danger I should have been aware of. I found out that he was having numerous affairs the entire time we were together. It's a miracle I didn't contract an STD or AIDS!"

False Belief #6: I Don't Have the Right to Stand Up for Myself or Act on My Own Behalf

Women have good reasons for not standing up for themselves. We have been conditioned to be passive, especially when it comes to relating to men. As mentioned earlier, until recently, many girls and women were completely dominated by their fathers and husbands. It was unheard of for a woman to stand up to a man, no matter how abusive he might be. It simply was not safe to fight back. For many women today, this is unfortunately still true.

We also need to remember that women have had to fight for the rights they now have—these rights were not given to us freely. It wasn't all that long ago that women couldn't vote. Such suffragists as Susan B. Anthony met in the 1840s to organize the American women's movement for the primary purpose of securing the right to vote. The false belief that women do not have a right to speak for or decide for themselves is a powerful remnant of our history as females.

For some women, this false belief also comes from their personal experiences of being dominated and/or abused. Although much has changed regarding the reporting of child abuse, countless girls are still dominated and abused in their homes. Standing up to an abusive parent is almost impossible for a child—and not usually a smart thing to do. And many girls learn by example, such as from a mother who is being verbally, emotionally, or physically abused by her partner, that standing up to the abuser only gets a woman into more trouble.

False Belief #7: Anger Is a Destructive Emotion and Shouldn't Be Expressed, Especially Directly to Those with Whom You Are Angry

This false belief is a very common and powerful one for many people, not just women. Those who were raised in an environment where there was one or more angry and/or violent adults often grow up believing that anger is dangerous and should be avoided at all costs. This was the case with Trudy, who was raised by a mother who had frequent, unexpected rages that she directed at whoever was around. Without much warning at all, Trudy's mother would suddenly start screaming and throwing objects around the room. Although Trudy's mother was mostly angry at her husband, the kids (there were five of them) were also the recipients of this rage if their mother felt they weren't listening to her or doing as she asked.

Trudy grew up to be a very mild-mannered woman who never got angry. She immersed herself in spirituality, joining a spiritually based commune right out of high school and marrying a man who shared her beliefs. She raised her children to be passive opponents of war and all types of violence, and she was a strong proponent of diplomacy in conflict resolution. Unfortunately, her husband did not practice his purported beliefs. He was a tyrant to her and to her children, expecting them to honor his every whim. In many ways, he treated his wife and the children as if they were his slaves. Fearful of experiencing his anger, Trudy silently went along with her husband's demands, no matter how unreasonable they were. It wasn't until he began to physically abuse her children that Trudy took action. She made a formal complaint about his behavior to the leaders of the commune, even though her husband was one of the leaders. This was very risky because she wasn't sure they would do anything and she would then anger her husband even more. Fortunately, the leaders took her complaint seriously and had a talk with her husband. He denied any such behavior on his part, but this did seem to curb his abusiveness for a while.

Although both men and women may have difficulties with the expression of anger, research tells us that parents and teachers discourage physical and direct aggression in girls early on, whereas anger in boys is either encouraged or ignored.

Rachel Simmons also found that there is still a definite double standard when it comes to aggression. Aggression is still seen as unfeminine and displays of aggression in females are punished with social rejection.

Girls and women continue to be socialized to avoid expressing their anger in direct or outward ways. In fact, "good girls" are not expected to experience anger at all. This is primarily because aggression imperils a girl's ability to be caring and nice; in other words, it undermines the image of what girls and women have been raised to become. Since girls are raised to be the caretakers and nurturers in relationships, aggression is discouraged in the belief that it endangers relationships.

False Belief #8: It Is Better to Avoid Conflict at All Costs

Girls are encouraged to identify with the nurturing behavior of their mothers. Many spend their childhood practicing the caretaking and nurturing of one another. Because they are expected to have perfect relationships with one another, girls are unprepared to negotiate conflict.

In a normal conflict, two people use language, their voices, or even their bodies to settle their dispute. The relationship between them is considered secondary to the issue being worked out. But with girls and women, the relationship is primary. They will do anything to preserve it—even if that means remaining silent and not expressing their hurt or anger. Because most girls and women have been discouraged, if not forbidden, to express anger, it goes underground. When anger cannot be voiced, and the skills to handle a conflict are absent, the problem that is causing their anger is never brought up and therefore never resolved.

Sociologist Anne Campbell, in her interviews with adults, found that whereas men viewed aggression as a means to control their environment and integrity, women believed showing it would terminate their relationships. Rachel Simmons discovered identical attitudes in her conversations with girls: "Expressing fear that even everyday acts of conflict, not to mention severe aggressive outbursts, would result in the loss of the people they most cared about, they refused to engage in even the most basic acts of conflict. Their equation was simple: conflict = loss."

Carol Gilligan found that girls equate danger in their lives with isolation. Most girls and women will do anything to avoid alienating someone they care for by not speaking up when they disagree with the person. For girls and women, the fear of being alone is overpowering. Many try to avoid being alone at all costs, even if it means remaining in an abusive friendship or romantic relationship.

As Simmons explained it, "In a world that socializes girls to prize relationships and care above all else, the fear of isolation and loss casts a long shadow over girls' decisions around conflicts, driving them away from direct confrontation." Many of the girls she interviewed expressed the fear that even everyday acts of conflict would result in the loss of the people they most cared about. A seventh grader explained, "If I tell my friends I'm angry with them, I'll have another enemy. It's a vicious cycle."

False Belief #9: There Is Good in Everyone, and If You Give Someone Enough Chances, He or She Will Eventually Show It to You

Women, far more than men, give people too many chances. This is often due to the expectation that girls and women be compassionate and forgiving. As nurturers and mothers, we are supposed to have infinite patience and tolerance. The fact is, we are biologically programmed to have these very qualities when it comes to our own children. When you think about it, the qualities of a good mother (or parent) include patience, tolerance, unconditional love, and for-giveness. So it is within our very nature to give people a second chance, to believe someone who tells us he or she won't do some-thing again or, at the very least, that he or she will try not to. But as women, we need to rein in this tendency. Giving someone a second chance is a good idea if the person has shown us in the past that he or she deserves it or if there is reason to believe the individual will, in fact, change. Otherwise, giving a second chance is usually a bad idea, especially when it comes to abusive behavior.

False Belief #10: Women Need Men to Protect Them and Support Them Financially

It is not surprising that women believe this. We have been condi-tioned to believe that we are the weaker sex and therefore need men to take care of us. Women feel especially vulnerable in the world, given the facts that we are generally not as physically strong as men and the world is becoming a more dangerous place every day. Women are more vulnerable than men: not only can we get mugged, we can get raped. As hundreds of thousands of rape victims know, an act of rape is so violent a violation that it can shatter the self-worth a woman has taken a lifetime to build.

But as mentioned earlier in the book, women can no longer depend on men to protect them or rescue them from danger. We must protect ourselves.

This includes being able to take care of ourselves financially. No matter what a woman's situation is—whether she is single or married—she needs to maintain her own bank account with enough savings that she is not dependent on a man for her livelihood. Unfortunately, many women end up staying with men they are unhappy with or who are abusive just because they don't have enough money to feel they have a voice in the household or to leave.

PART TWO

FROM FALSE BELIEFS TO EMPOWERING BELIEFS

4

Stop Putting Others' Feelings and Needs ahead of Your Own

I have another duty equally sacred. . . .
My duty to myself.
—HENRIK IBSEN, *A DOLL'S HOUSE*

False belief: Other people's feelings and needs are more important than my own.

Empowering belief: My feelings and needs are just as important as anyone else's.

This chapter is especially beneficial for
Martyrs

Women are biologically programmed to be caretakers. Add this to the fact that many women are socialized from early childhood to put other people first and to sacrifice for the people they care about, and we find that it is not uncommon for women to put other people's feelings and needs ahead of their own. Most psychologists would agree that the average woman is more willing to compromise her beliefs, values, and desires to maintain a relationship than is the average man.

Unfortunately, putting other people's feelings and needs ahead of her own can create a situation in which a woman actually becomes unaware of or numb to her own feelings and needs. Once this occurs, she is a prime candidate to be used or abused by others without her even realizing it. She becomes so focused outside of herself and so cut off from her own needs that, in essence, she neglects and abuses herself.

Even the most liberated and powerful women can fall into the trap of putting others' needs and feelings first. In *Revolution from Within*, Gloria Steinem wrote about her own experience of being what she called "empathy sick," meaning that she had focused so much of her time and attention on helping others and meeting their needs that she had lost touch with herself and her own needs. She reached a point when she knew other people's feelings better than her own.

In my book *Loving Him without Losing You*, I wrote about my own experience with empathy sickness. About fifteen years ago, I became burned out physically, emotionally, and spiritually from spending all my time and energy on helping clients and pouring my soul into one relationship after another. Both my physical and emotional health were suffering, and I had lost touch with my own needs.

This is a typical scenario for many women—not just those who are committed to social change and the betterment of others. Women tend to focus so much attention on caring for others, on being empathetic to the needs of others, that we get lost in the process.

Self-Blame

Another issue women experience is that they tend to blame themselves for problems in their relationships. For example, if a woman's husband constantly complains that she is not meeting his needs, she doesn't question whether he is being too critical or demanding. Instead, she will probably bend over backward to please him. This was the situation with my client Rhonda, who had been married for five years when she came to see me. She had become very depressed and wasn't sure why. As she explained during our first session, "I'm so disappointed in myself. I just can't seem to get it together. My husband says I'm lazy, and I guess he's right. After all, I can't seem to do even the simplest task correctly."

She explained that her husband, Matt, had a strong need for order in the house. "I know he likes things just a certain way. That's the way he was raised. His mother was an immaculate housekeeper. I've tried to do a good job with the house, but I keep on falling short, no matter how hard I try."

I wanted to know what it was that didn't please her husband. "Well, I can't seem to keep the kitchen clean enough. He's always finding spots on the appliances. And he spent a lot of money having new hardwood floors put in, and I keep spilling water on them when I water the plants. He likes his underwear and pajamas washed and folded a certain way and I just can't seem to do it right. I either put in too much fabric softener or too little. And even though he taught me the right way to fold the laundry, I'm just not as good at it as he is."

When I asked Rhonda whether she thought her husband was too particular, she said, "I guess some people might say that he is, but these things are important to him. As he tells me all the time, if I really love him I should want to do these things for him. I should be able to learn how to do them right so he'll be happy."

Rhonda had become so focused on pleasing her husband that she had lost touch with reality. The truth was that her husband's demands were unreasonable. Not only was he too particular, he was browbeating her mercilessly whenever she failed to please him—which was most of the time. Rhonda was being emotionally abused.

As is the case with most women who are being emotionally abused, Rhonda blamed herself rather than recognizing that her husband was impossible to please and that he had an investment in keeping her down and off balance. Had she not been so focused on meeting his needs, she would have become aware of the fact that his emotional abuse was affecting her self-esteem and making her depressed.

Other Blind Spots

Still another problem is that if you are overly focused on pleasing others, you can be blind to the fact that you are involved with someone who is self-absorbed or narcissistic. Beth came into therapy because she was involved with a man for over a year yet he had never told her he loved her. She wanted to know if she was doing something wrong that might be turning him off.

From Beth's description of her current relationship, everything has been going really well. Since she didn't really have a strong point of view on things, she explained, she was more than happy to listen to Cliff's opinions and to agree with him on most issues. Since she didn't think her life was all that interesting, she was thrilled to listen to his adventures.

"I know he must care about me; otherwise, why would he want to be around me?" she shared with me during one of our sessions. But from Beth's description, I surmised that Cliff was narcissistic. He seemed to be very wrapped up in himself and didn't show much interest in Beth or what went on in her life. It seemed to be all about him. When I pointed this out to Beth, she immediately made excuses for him: "Oh, he just likes to talk a lot more than I do. I'm just not a big talker. And he's so much more interesting than I am."

As I got to know Beth better, she admitted that she had often been taken advantage of by previous boyfriends and even by some women friends. She admitted to me that both men and women often told her that she was easy to be around and she suspected it was because she let them have their way and didn't insist on their paying attention to her needs. Beth needed to learn that until she put her needs first, she was always going to attract people who were either users, abusers, or those like Cliff, who were narcissistic.

As I was to learn later on, however, Beth didn't even know what her needs were. She was so used to focusing outside herself that she didn't know what she was feeling or what she needed at any given time. Instead, she spent most of her time and energy trying to please others.

Nice Girls Also Become Resentful

Women who consistently defer to the needs and feelings of others experience yet another problem: they become resentful and angry toward the very people they strive to please. Nice Girls often expect others to be as considerate and self-sacrificing as they are, only to become disappointed and resentful when those people don't come through.

Even more problematic, some Nice Girls become resentful of others who *do* take care of themselves and put their own needs first. This happens most often with Nice Girls who are married and/or mothers. My client Sheila was a case in point. Sheila often complained that her husband, Derrick, was selfish. "All he does is think of himself. He makes sure that he gets plenty of time to do the things he wants to do. For example, instead of getting up and helping to get the kids ready for school, he gets up early and goes for a run. By the time he's back, the kids are already at school. On the weekend, no matter what else we have planned as a family, he always manages to carve out enough time to go play golf."

Although some people truly are selfish or do not keep up their end of the bargain in terms of helping out with the kids or with household chores, a great deal of the problem really centers around the fact that Nice Girls don't assert their right to take care of their own needs. Sheila's problem wasn't that her husband was selfish; it was that she was not selfish *enough*. The truth was, she envied his ability to take care of his own needs because she lacked the courage and the ability to take care of her own.

My work with Sheila centered around helping her to get over the guilt feelings she experienced whenever she took time for herself. Instead of her "asking permission" to go to the gym, I helped her to simply state her intention: "I need to start going back to the gym. Let's work out a plan so I can do it."

Childhood Messages

Parental messages can also set women up to be self-sacrificing. As Sheila and I worked together to help her set aside her belief that other people's feelings and needs were more important than her own, I began to feel that in addition to the cultural conditioning that all girls experience, something more powerful was going on with Sheila. I asked her if she remembered anyone telling her that she was selfish if she put her own needs first. Sheila's eyes got very big and she immediately said, "My mother told me that all the time." She explained that her mother always complained to her that Sheila always had time to do things for herself but never enough time to help her clean the house.

I sat silently looking at Sheila, hoping she realized that she said the very same things to her husband. But she was lost in her memory of her mother's words. "I think that's where I got the idea that I was selfish and self-absorbed," she said quietly.

Sheila explained that she really wanted to prove her mother wrong, and so she went out of her way to be caring and concerned for other people. "I always put myself in the other person's shoes and asked myself how they must feel. I probably also did this because I didn't feel like my mother cared about my feelings. I guess a lot of my life has been about proving my mother wrong and making sure that I wasn't like her."

Role Reversal and Parentified Children

Another reason some Nice Girls focus much of their attention on the needs of others is that they were raised by parents who insisted they put those parents' needs first. What are commonly referred to as "parentified" children constantly receive messages about what they are supposed to be doing for their parents. The messages and expectations are so internalized that even when they reach adulthood, they tend to respond to others in the same way they responded (and continue to respond) to their parents.

As Nina Brown, author of *Children of the Self-Absorbed*, put it: "Children who have to assume a parent's role often have done so from a very early age and don't know any other way of being. They are so conditioned that they assume their experience is universal. Even when they become aware of other ways of being and behaving, they are frequently unable to break away from the early conditioning."

In many cases, a parent may simply be unable to be emotionally or physically available for his or her child. Children can also become parentified when a parent is depressed or chronically ill (including being emotionally disturbed or mentally ill). In all of these situations, the parent is not able to meet the child's needs and has become so needy that the child is forced to assume the parent's role. The child is expected to meet the parent's needs for attention, admiration, and emotional connectedness. In such cases, the child is given the message that his or her needs are not as important as the parents'.

Remedies

Remedy #1: Discover the Origin of Your Tendency to Put Other People's Feelings and Needs Ahead of Your Own

As I explained earlier, most women's Nice Girl beliefs and behaviors stem from four major sources: biological, societal, familial, and experiential. To stop putting other people's feelings and needs ahead of your own, it is important for you to determine where this false belief originated for you.

If you have only a slight tendency to focus on the feelings and needs of others, you may suffer from what most women experience as they are growing up—a biological predisposition and the societal message that women should be compassionate and empathetic caretakers. If you have a stronger tendency, it may be that you were taught to be self-sacrificing by your parents—either because they gave you this overt message or because you witnessed one parent (probably your mother) sacrificing herself for her husband and children.

But if you suffer from a strong *need* to focus on others to the exclusion of listening to your own needs and feelings, it may be that you had self-absorbed or narcissistic parents or an alcoholic parent, or that you were emotionally, physically, or sexually abused as a child. Victims of sexual abuse, in particular, learn the powerful message that the perpetrator's needs and feelings were all that mattered and that their own needs and feelings were unimportant.

It often takes some soul-searching to discover the origin of your tendency to put your needs aside. The following example provides you with a model for this self-exploration.

Patricia: A Model for Self-Exploration

Patricia came to see me because she was concerned about her husband's drinking and how it would affect her two children. For the past four years, she had been coming out of denial about just how much of a drinking problem her husband had. She told me that she had put up with inappropriate behavior from him for a long time but was now unwilling to continue to expose her children to it. "I can put up with his behavior, even though it embarrasses me and makes me angry. But I don't want my kids to have to see it."

In spite of Patricia's resolve to end the relationship, she was having a very difficult time following through. "I don't want to hurt him. I know he'll be devastated. We've been together for a long time and he isn't really close to anyone else. I know he's going to end up all alone and I hate for that to happen. If it wasn't for the kids, I'd just put up with him."

As we talked more, Patricia revealed that she hadn't felt much love for her husband for some time. "It didn't start out this way. I was crazy about him for the longest time. But I gradually lost any feeling for him because of the way he treats me. My friends and family can't understand why I've stayed with him for so long. They all saw what I am just beginning to see—just how selfish and cruel he can be. They all think I deserve to be with someone who treats me with a lot more respect."

I asked Patricia why she would be willing to basically accept a situation that was obviously unacceptable. "I just don't want to hurt him. I'm one of those people who would rather be hurt than hurt someone else." When I asked why this was so, she answered, "I don't know, I've always been that way."

As is often the case, I felt that the best way to help Patricia was to explore her childhood. She explained that her father was a very loving man and she was extremely close to him. This was partly due to the fact that she felt sorry for him because her mother was a very dominant and demanding woman who ordered him around constantly. As a child, Patricia wanted to protect her father from her mother, but of course, she really couldn't. Instead, she took care of her father in every way she could. She brought him his newspaper and a bottle of beer when he came home. Whenever Patricia's mother would yell at him, Patricia would sit next to him or give him a hug or rub his feet to make him feel better.

But as kind and loving as Patricia's father was, he was also an alcoholic. As the years went by, he became worse and worse. Although he always managed to go to work, he got drunk every night and typically passed out on the couch. He was less and less available to Patricia, and by the time she was in high school they seldom connected at all. Nevertheless, as far as she was concerned, he was the greatest father a girl could have.

When I probed further about how her father's alcoholism affected her, Patricia visibly squirmed in her chair. "I'm sure it's had its affect. I've had a problem with drinking too much myself in the past. And I did marry an alcoholic, after all," she offered.

"How about the fact that you ended up taking care of your father instead of the other way around?" I asked.

Patricia gave me a blank look and quickly said, "Oh, he took care of me. He was a very good provider. He managed to pay for my college even though he didn't make all that much money."

I could see that even though Patricia was clear about the role her father's alcoholism had in her marrying an alcoholic, she was in denial about how her taking care of him had turned her into a Nice Girl.

"From my perspective it seems to me that, when you were a child, you were so focused on taking care of your father and protecting him from your mother that you didn't take care of your own needs, or even know what they were. Can you see that?" I asked her quietly.

Again, Patricia gave me a blank look, but I could tell that the wheels were spinning. "I've never thought of that. I guess I should have, but I just never saw it that way." She fell silent and I allowed her to stay with her own feelings. When she spoke again she said, "This really is a pattern in my life. I've been this way with other men, too, other people actually. I always go along with whatever other people want to do. I don't really think about my own needs."

This was a huge breakthrough for Patricia. She needed time to integrate the information but she had faced a core issue. During our next session, I asked her if she felt any anger toward her father.

"It's difficult. I felt so sorry for him because of my mother. I always felt he drank as a way to cope with her. But I've been thinking about it since our last appointment, and I'm beginning to see that he was responsible for putting up with her in the first place— just as I am responsible for putting up with my husband. I can see how I even started drinking too much to cope with my husband. But I love my kids so much that I didn't want them to have an alcoholic mother *and* father so I went to AA and stopped drinking. It was very hard, but I did it for them. My father could have done the same for me."

Patricia was quiet again for quite some time, and I could see that this was the way she processed her feelings. She was a very introspective person and was doing really good work.

"I guess I never wanted to hold my father responsible for anything. He was so kind and sweet to me. But he was responsible. And just being nice and sweet doesn't cut it, does it?" Patricia flashed me a knowing smile to show me that she got the connection.

I encouraged Patricia to write down her emerging feelings about her father in her journal. I also asked her to pay attention to any feelings of anger that might bubble up as she faced more and more about her father, and to find a healthy and constructive way of releasing that anger. I suggested she write her father a letter expressing her anger and assured her that she didn't need to give it to him. I also suggested she give herself permission to release her anger in a physical way, such as putting her head against a pillow and screaming, or using her fists to hit her bed.

The next time I saw Patricia, she had a lot more energy than she had during our first two visits. "I can't believe how much better I feel. I still have a lot of work to do. I'm still not ready to walk out on my husband tomorrow but I'm a lot closer to ending it. It's taken me a long time to face the truth about all this, but now that I have I feel more motivated than ever to get my kids away from him—at least on a full-time basis. I don't want them to grow up like I did."

Patricia also reported that she had written about her feelings about her father in her journal. "It's still really hard for me to do. I still want to protect him. I find myself making excuses for him, but then I think about my kids. I think about how I put them in the same situation I was in as a kid. I think about how they have already been hurt by having an alcoholic for a father and by seeing their mother put up with someone who is so cruel."

"And can you get angry for how you suffered? Can you get in touch with how it must have felt for you to take care of your father instead of having him take care of you?" I asked.

"I'm beginning to. I still try to convince myself that he was a great father, and in some ways he was. But now I'm allowing myself to remember the bad times—like when he'd be falling down drunk in front of my friends, and how I'd come home from a date to find him passed out on the couch in his underwear."

Patricia had come a long way. Her first step was in discovering the origins of her tendency to put the feelings and needs of others ahead of her own. I'll talk more later in this chapter about how you can continue to come out of denial about your own childhood experiences, how you can come to acknowledge and release your anger, and what parentified children need to do to recover.

Remedy #2: Look Deeper at Your Tendency to Be Resentful or Angry at Those Who Do Take Care of Themselves

Many Nice Girls are envious of others who take good care of themselves. Although they are not consciously aware of this, it is because they secretly wish they could take better care of themselves. Many claim that they don't have the time, due to a heavy workload or their having children to raise. Others blame their spouses for not helping them more. But the truth is, your reason for not taking better care of yourself lies within you. No matter how busy you are, how neglectful your partner is, or how many children you have to raise, you can still find time to take care of yourself if you put your mind to it.

Earlier I mentioned that I had hoped that Sheila would make the connection between the way she talked to and about her husband and the way her mother had talked to her, and eventually she did. This happened during one of our sessions. As she tended to do, she began by complaining about how selfish Derrick was. I sympathized with how he did not do his share when it came to childcare and helping around the house, a common complaint about husbands, many of whom see that as "women's work." I also reminded Sheila that Derrick did make a good living for the family—a good enough living that she was able to be a stay-at-home mom—and that he was a good and decent man in many respects. She didn't have the ideal husband but she certainly didn't have the worst.

She responded with, "I know, I know. But I just hate it that he has so much freedom, while I feel like a prisoner in my own home sometimes. I hate it that he takes such good care of his body when I don't ever have the time to work out or get a massage."

When I suggested to her that she could, in fact, make time for herself, she balked. "But I always feel selfish when I do that. I always hear my mother's voice, 'You have time to do your nails but you don't have time to clean the kitchen.'" This time she got it. "Oh my God, that's exactly how I talk to my husband. I'm always saying to him, 'You have time to go for a run but you don't have time to help me with the kids.' No wonder I resent him. He's doing what I want to do but don't because I don't want to look selfish. I resent him because he doesn't seem to feel guilty like I was made to feel. In fact, I've been trying to make him feel guilty."

Sheila had taken a huge step. Now she needed to realize that taking care of herself, doing things for herself, was not selfish. She needed to realize that she had a *right* to think of her own needs. You probably need to do the same thing.

Remedy #3: Come to Believe That It Is Not Selfish to Think of Your Own Needs First

Because of all your prior conditioning, you may believe that taking care of yourself is a selfish act. But your highest responsibility is to yourself. When you take care of your own needs first, you will be able to be a genuinely caring, giving person, not a martyr thinking everyone owes her something or a victim begrudging all that she gives. Although it may be uncomfortable at first, and you may be afraid that others won't like you unless you cater to their needs first, keep trying. Eventually, you will find that nothing bad happens to you just because you think of yourself first or because you do what *you* want to do.

You've heard it before: if you don't take care of yourself, you won't be able to take care of others. Even the airlines know this. That's why they instruct you to put on your own oxygen mask before putting on your child's.

If your basic needs for nurturing, protection, and support were not met by neglectful or self-absorbed parents, you will have a particularly difficult time knowing how to meet those needs now. It is as if there is a disconnect inside you between what you need and providing it for yourself. A child needs to receive love to be able to feel love. This includes love for oneself. If we do not love ourselves, we will not be motivated to take care of ourselves. Those who were neglected or emotionally abused often look at those who are motivated to take care of themselves with wonder. "Where do they get the motivation?" they ask themselves. "Why do they care so much about their health or the way they look?" They are poignantly aware that there is something missing inside themselves, something that creates the kind of motivation that would cause someone to say no to a piece of cake, the kind of motivation to get up at six o'clock in the morning in order to get to the gym before going to work, the kind of motivation that would help someone leave an abusive partner. The something that is missing is self-love.

Some adults who were neglected or emotionally abused do not take care of themselves because they feel they do not deserve it. Children tend to blame the neglect and abuse they experience on themselves, in essence saying to themselves, "My mother is treating me like this because I've been bad" or "I am being neglected because I am unlovable." Adult survivors tend to continue this kind of rationalization, believing that they are to blame for their own deprivation and abuse as children. As adults, they put up with poor treatment by friends, relatives, and romantic partners because they believe they brought it on themselves. When good things happen to them, they may actually become uncomfortable. They feel so unworthy that they cannot take in the good.

EXERCISE: WHY DO YOU NOT TAKE BETTER CARE OF YOURSELF?

- Write down the reason or reasons you believe you do not take better care of yourself.

- What beliefs do you have about your right to take care of yourself?

- List all the ways that you deprive yourself of nurturing, support, protection, and so forth.

Remedy #4: Create a Positive and Powerful Statement

No matter how you were raised or what you believe about taking care of yourself, you can begin to change.

- Create what Laurel Mellin, the author of *The Pathway*, calls a positive and powerful statement that will counter your negative belief that it is not okay to take care of your own needs. For example, it may be as simple as: "It is okay to take care of my own needs first." Or, you may need to remind yourself that you *deserve* to take care of yourself or that you have a *right* to do so. In that case, your positive and powerful statement might be: "I deserve to consider my own needs first," or "I have the right to think of my own needs." Or, you may have to remind yourself that you need to take care of yourself in order to let go of your tendency to be a martyr—"I have an obligation to myself and to others to take care of my own needs first."

- Work on your positive and powerful statement until it feels right—until it really *resonates* with you emotionally. It needs to be something that you can believe or that you are willing to believe in time.

- Make a point of repeating this positive and powerful statement several times a day. Do what Mellin suggests and "grind it in," meaning that you repeat it until you begin to believe it (she recommends you repeat it ten times, three times a day).

- Don't just say the words mindlessly, really *feel* them as you say them. Let the words permeate your very being. Take a deep breath and take the words into your body, mind, and spirit.

Remedy #5: Discover or Rediscover What Your Needs Are

Because you have been focused primarily on the needs of others, your own needs have probably gone unmet. What makes matters worse is that you probably don't even know what your own needs are. This may be because you simply haven't paid attention to them or because your needs may have been ignored when you were a child and, as an adult, you have continued to ignore them. (As adults, we often treat ourselves the way we were treated as a children.)

Once you have identified your real needs, you will be better able to meet them. The following exercise will help you determine what your needs are.

EXERCISE: OUR BASIC NEEDS

1. Take a close look at the following list of basic needs and think about how often you satisfy these needs for yourself.

Hunger: Give yourself healthy food to eat.

Thirst: Give yourself plenty of water—not diet or sweet drinks, but water.

Sleep: Go to bed at a reasonable time; don't eat before bed or take any stimulants.

Companionship: Don't allow yourself to become isolated. Reach out when you are lonely.

Sex: Provide yourself with healthy outlets for sex, neither depriving nor indulging yourself.

Stimulation: Get involved in activities that stimulate your mind, body, and spirit.

Spiritual connection: Satisfy your need for contemplation, gratitude, prayer, ritual, or any other type of spiritual expression you need.

2. Make a list of the needs you are meeting and how you are meeting them.

3. List the needs that have gone unmet and think of ways that you can begin to meet them.

Remedy #6: Make the Connection between Needs and Feelings

One way of discovering what your needs are at any given time is to check in with your feelings. Your feelings will tell you what you are lacking, if you pay close attention. Unfortunately, many Nice Girls are as out of touch with their feelings as they are with their needs and have difficulty identifying what emotions they are experiencing. This may be a direct result of focusing on the feelings of others too much, or of having been a means of surviving childhood experiences such as neglect or trauma. Because of this, you may now experience such a jumble of feelings that you have difficulty identifying them or you may as an adult be numb to your feelings.

In the course of just one day, we all experience myriad emotions. Learning to identify each and every one of them can be a daunting task. Therefore, it is best to focus on only a few primary emotions, at least in the beginning. According to most experts, there are eight or so primary, or basic, emotions: anger, sorrow, joy, surprise, fear, disgust, guilt/shame, and interest (some also consider love one of the primary emotions). These are considered primary emotions because we are born with the potential, or biological readiness, for them. All other emotions are considered secondary, or social, emotions because they are learned. These are usually some combination of the basic emotions. For our purposes, we are going to focus on five of the primary emotions: anger, sadness, fear, guilt/shame, and joy.

We often become disconnected from our primary emotions by diluting them and giving them other names. For example, many people, instead of saying they are afraid, will say they feel "anxious" or "worried." Instead of saying they feel sad (or even knowing they are sad), many people will say they feel "tired." And instead of saying they are angry, many people will say they are "uninterested," "bored," or "frustrated."

The best way to discover how you are feeling is to begin by asking yourself which of the five primary feelings you are experiencing (anger, sadness, fear, guilt/shame, or joy) at intervals throughout the day. It is safe to say that at any given time, we are all experiencing at least one or more of these primary emotions.

Remedy #7: Reconnect with Your Body

Just asking yourself which feeling you are experiencing won't necessarily help, if you aren't in touch with your body. Your body is your best barometer to tell you which emotion you are feeling at any given time. Emotions involve body changes, such as fluctuations in heart rate and skin temperature, and the tensing or relaxing of muscles. The most important changes are in the facial muscles. Researchers now think that changes in the facial muscles play an important role in actually causing emotions. For example, we tend to feel sadness in our body in the following ways: frowning or a mouth turned down in a "sad" face; eyes drooping; a slumped, hunched posture; using a low, quiet, slow, or monotonous voice; heaviness in the chest; tightness in the throat or difficulty swallowing (from holding back tears); moist eyes or tears; whimpering, crying, tears; feeling as if you can't stop crying or that if you ever start crying you will never stop; feeling tired, run-down, or low in energy; feeling lethargic, listless; wanting to stay in bed all day; feeling as if nothing is pleasurable anymore; feeling a pain or hollowness in your chest or gut; feeling empty.

Conversely, joy is usually manifested in the body in the following ways: smiling; feeling excited; feeling physically energetic, active, "alive"; feeling like laughing or giggling; having a warm glow about you; feeling "open hearted" and loving.

EXERCISE: CHECKING IN WITH YOUR BODY

1. Look in the mirror and notice what expression you have on your face. Does your face look angry? Sad? Afraid?

2. Now sit down and take a few deep breaths

3. Check in with your body. What emotion is being expressed there? If there is heaviness in your chest, what emotion might that be? If there is an uneasiness in your stomach, what might that be saying about how you are feeling?

4. Notice any tension in your body—in your shoulders, your neck, your jaw, your stomach, your hands.

5. Take a few more deep breaths and ask yourself what emotion is connected to this tension. Is it anger? Fear? Sadness?

6. Now, taking the information you have gathered both from the expression on your face and the tension in your body, what emotions do you think you are feeling?

Remedy #8: Make It a Practice of Checking In with Your Feelings Several Times a Day

Start by making sure you check in with your feelings at least once a day. The best times are when you get up in the morning and when you go to bed. You can even do it when you are driving to and from someplace (as long as your emotions don't become so strong that they interfere with your driving).

Take a few minutes to center yourself. Take some deep breaths and clear your mind of any thoughts. Go inside yourself and ask yourself, "What am I feeling?" For simplicity's sake, check for the following emotions: anger, sadness, fear, and guilt.

1. Start by asking yourself, "Am I feeling angry?" Check in with yourself and allow any angry feelings you might have to surface. If the answer is yes, simply list (in your head, out

loud, or on paper) the reasons you are feeling this way. For example, "I'm angry that _____." Or "I'm angry because _____." If the answer is "no," proceed to the next emotion.

2. Now ask yourself, "Am I feeling sad?" Again, allow the feelings of sadness to bubble up and list all the reasons you feel sad.

3. The next question is, "Am I feeling afraid?" Allow the feelings of fear to come up if they are there. If they are not, go on to the next feeling.

4. Ask yourself, "Am I feeling guilty?" Allow the feelings to surface and list all the reasons you feel guilty.

5. You do not need to do anything about the feelings that have surfaced. The point of the check-in is to help you to keep in touch with your feelings.

Remedy #9: Connect Your Feelings with Your Needs

Now you are ready to connect your feelings with your needs. The following exercise, based on a process by Laurel Mellin in her Solutions Program, will help you make the connection.

EXERCISE: FEELINGS AND NEEDS

1. Check in with yourself several times a day by going inside and asking yourself what you are feeling.

2. When you find a feeling, look for the corresponding need. Ask yourself, "What do I need?" Often the answer will be, "Feel my feeling and let it fade." Answer in the simplest way instead of confusing the issue with too many details or complexities. For example, if you are hungry, you need food. When you feel guilty, you need to apologize.

3. It may take trying on several needs before you find the one that is true for you. You may also have many needs attached to one feeling. For example, if you feel lonely, your need may be to call a friend, to get a hug from your partner, to connect with yourself.

4. Be on the alert for answers that are not truly responsive to you. For example, "I feel sad, therefore I need some candy," or "I feel angry, so I need to hit him." Tap into your inherent wisdom and relax into a more logical, self-nurturing answer. Ask yourself, "Okay, what do I really need?" For example, "Express myself (write, sing)," "Get physical (walk, stomp)," "Develop a plan," "Learn from it (next time I will _____)."

Remedy #10: Stop Treating Yourself the Way Your Parents Treated You

Many Nice Girls deprive, abandon, control, shame, or ignore themselves just as their parents did to them. You may be so used to being deprived that you continue to deprive yourself. You may be so used to being ignored that you ignore yourself.

For instance, if you were neglected as a child or if you were given the message that your own needs didn't matter and that you should always put other people's needs first, you may now neglect yourself. This is because we often treat ourselves the way we were treated as children. In fact, as adults, we often treat ourselves *worse* than we were treated while growing up.

An important aspect of self-care is discovering all the ways you treat yourself the way your parents treated you as a child.

EXERCISE: HOW YOU NEGLECT AND DEPRIVE YOURSELF THE WAY YOUR PARENTS DID

1. Make a list of the ways you neglect or deprive yourself of what you need.

2. Write down every example you can think of regarding how your parents neglected to take care of you. Include ways they deprived you emotionally, as well as physically.

3. Take a close look at your list and see if there is a connection between the way you treat yourself today and how you were treated by your parents.

You do not have to stay trapped in repeating the depriving behavior you learned from your parents. You can become the responsive, nurturing parent to yourself that you deserved all along.

Remedy #11: Discover What Focusing on Others Does for You Today

The reason women began focusing on others in the first place may have come from their past conditioning, but there are also reasons they continue this behavior today. In other words, there is a payoff for continuing to focus outside of ourselves. One of the main reasons is that often, by focusing on the needs of others, we can avoid facing what we are feeling. This is particularly true whenever we obsess about someone else, such as a partner or a child. In fact, it is safe to say that whenever we are obsessing about anything, we are avoiding ourselves. For this reason, I suggest you do the following whenever you find yourself worrying about someone else constantly. Ask yourself these two questions: "What am I trying to avoid?" and "What am I feeling?"

The following exercise will also help you discover the payoffs you can experience whenever you focus outside of yourself.

EXERCISE: PAYOFFS TO FOCUSING OUTSIDE OF YOURSELF

1. Take some time to think about what you get out of focusing on others more than on yourself or to the exclusion of yourself. For example, one answer that may come to you is that it is just a habit. That is a valid answer but try to dig a bit deeper to find some actual *payoffs*—specific benefits that you experience when you focus outside of yourself.

2. Make a list of the reasons that you come up with. This may be difficult at first but keep working on it until you come up with some answers. The following example of reasons written by my client Lily may help give you some ideas:

   - It is a habit. I just do it automatically without thinking.
   - It makes me feel good to help someone else.
   - I think it is selfish and self-centered to think of myself.
   - I don't think my needs are important.

Now I invite you to go even deeper to examine the *benefits* of focusing on the needs and feelings of others or for your caretaking behavior. Here is what my client Lily wrote:

- I realize that one of the reasons I feel good when I help someone else is that it makes me feel superior to them.

- I also realize that thinking about others keeps me from paying attention to myself. I am constantly critical of myself, always finding fault. Focusing on others gives me a break from my negative self-talk.

- I somehow need to justify my existence and I do this by helping others. I have so much self-doubt, so many feelings of not being "okay," and helping others temporarily takes those feelings away.

Remedy #12: Start Giving to Yourself What You Give to Others

Contrary to the old saying, "Do unto others as you would have them do unto you," Nice Girls need to start treating themselves the way they treat others.

1. Make a list of all the things you do for those you love, especially acts of kindness and nurturing (examples: "I make sure I tell my daughter how proud I am of her," "My husband likes clean sheets so I change our sheets a lot more often than I normally would."

2. Now list the reasons for your doing these things (examples: "My mother never told me she was proud of me and I don't want my daughter to doubt herself the way I did." "It makes my husband feel loved for me to go out of my way to change the sheets.")

3. Go over your list and think of similar ways you can nurture and take care of yourself. In the previous examples, the answers might be: "I need to think of reasons to be proud of myself and allow myself to feel that pride." "I really feel good when I have a manicure and pedicure. It really raises my spirits every time I look at my nails. I need to give myself the gift of having an appointment every week."

Note that if you are involved with an abusive partner, there is something you need to understand: abusive people insist that their partners focus on their needs. The main way out of the abusive cycle is for you to reorient your thinking so that you devote your attention to yourself and your children. You need to stop trying to appease the abuser and turn your energy toward yourself.

Remedy #13: Think of Your Need to Focus on Others as an Addiction

One reason it is so difficult to give up focusing on others' needs and feelings is that helping others can result in immediate rewards. People respond positively to those who are kind, considerate, and selfless. They show their appreciation by smiling at you, thanking you, telling you what a wonderful, caring person you are. It also feels good to do things for other people. As Sheila put it, "It's such a win in the moment." But just like any addiction, the good feelings usually don't last very long before you need another fix. In addition, just as it was with Sheila, if you *don't* get the acknowledgment you need, you may start to get resentful.

Like giving up any addiction, it is going to be difficult to stop putting other people's feelings and needs first. It has become automatic for you to put yourself last. That is why you need to create a routine, a practice of meeting your own needs. The more you repeat this new pattern, the more likely it, too, will become automatic. The habit of doing daily or even hourly "feelings checks" is a good place to start.

Remedy #14: Make a Commitment to Begin Meeting Your Needs

Often, in order for us to take the action needed to create a real change in our lives, we need to make a commitment. This commitment needs to be a promise we make to ourselves—not to anyone else—that we will do something *no matter what*. We can't put it off, we can't make excuses for not doing it—we are *committed* to doing it.

1. Start by thinking about what you wanted from your parents but didn't receive. For example, did you want their encour-

agement? Their approval? Did you crave more affection? Make a list of all the things you wished you had received from your parents but did not.

2. List the ways you plan to start giving to yourself what your parents didn't give to you. For example, if you didn't receive encouragement, write on your list that you will begin to encourage yourself.

3. Make a commitment to immediately begin doing one concrete thing that will provide you with what you missed as a child.

As you can see, I've listed many remedies in this chapter—more than in any other chapter, as a matter of fact. This is because learning to put your needs ahead of others' needs is one of the most difficult habits for Nice Girls to break. You may not need every remedy listed, but take your time and address each remedy that applies to you.

5

Stop Believing That Being Nice Will Protect You

Life isn't fair.

—UNKNOWN

False belief: If I am nice (and fair) to other people they will be nice (and fair) to me.

Empowering belief: I can protect myself and be fair to myself.

*This chapter is especially beneficial for
Prudes, Enlightened Ones*

Nice Girls believe that the way to protect themselves from being hurt, rejected, or abandoned by others is to be supernice to everyone. They believe that if they just don't rock the boat, if they smile sweetly and agree with everyone, no one will get angry with them or be mean to them. In other words, Nice Girls use being nice as a protective shield.

Where Did We Get the Idea That Being Nice Would Protect Us?

Once again, we need to remind ourselves of our history as women to fully understand this way of thinking. It wasn't all that long ago that women were considered property—first of their father and then their husband. Their safety and welfare depended on the goodwill of men. If a girl or a woman was not nice to the men in her life, she was punished, rejected, or even abandoned by them. Much like the black slaves in the South, women learned to be nice—pleasant, polite, gracious, agreeable, and compliant—to survive. I believe we hold the memories of these not-so-distant times in our collective memories and in our very cells.

Another source of the false belief that being nice will protect you from being hurt by others is the concept of "magical thinking"—the idea that thoughts are as potent as actions. Young children often use the innate tendency toward magical thinking to ward off fears and to gain an illusion of control over what happens to them. A good example of childlike magical thinking is believing that if you are good and do all the things your parents ask you to do, they won't get a divorce. It is easy to understand how the belief that "being nice" can ward off harm could be created in a child's mind.

Around the age of seven or eight, children normally learn that there is a difference between wishing and making something happen in reality. By puberty, most magical thinking has been transformed into reality-based plans and action or into culturally acceptable forms, including faith and prayer. However, some childlike ways of thinking—some magical thoughts—can stay with us even as adults, especially when such thoughts provide relief from fear and anxiety. Even when we examine these magical thoughts logically and realize they are no longer true, we may still secretly hold onto them.

This is particularly true when a painful or traumatic childhood experience is associated with the belief in the protective power of niceness. For example, a child may believe that by being nice, he or she can actually prevent something bad from happening, or, conversely, that by doing or thinking something that was not nice, he or she actually *caused* the bad thing to happen.

Believing in Fairness Is Also Magical Thinking

The magical thinking that being nice will shield you from harm is closely related to the idea that life is fair or that it ought to be: the view that being nice is protective is firmly grounded in the core expectation that life is fair.

The belief that life is fair is a childhood fantasy. It, too, is magical thinking rooted in a conviction that we can control what happens with our minds and our behavior. For a time, children need that innocent belief that everything happens for a reason and that they have power and control over their lives. Without this illusion, they would be overwhelmed by a world that feels unpredictable and unmanageable. Even as adults, we want some reassurance that we have some control over the events of our lives.

But if we scratch the surface of our illusions, we find fear. It is a fear rooted in childhood—a fear of abandonment, rejection, and, ultimately, death. We carry our childhood beliefs into our adult lives to ward off the reality of how little control and power we actually have.

The dilemma that Nice Girls often face is that when the world doesn't work the way it should, when life isn't fair and people hurt them even though they are nice, they become confused and frustrated. They also feel angry because their expectations of how others *should* treat them when they are nice are not being met. Of course, Nice Girls are too nice to direct that anger toward others who may have wronged them. Instead, they are more likely to turn that anger inward, against themselves, and to blame themselves for not being nice enough or for deserving the mistreatment for some other reason. In that way, they can hold onto their false beliefs and life remains fair in their minds.

This kind of magical thinking can set you up for self-blame and recrimination. If you continue to believe that others will be nice to you if you are nice to them, you are left with thinking that you have only yourself to blame when others let you down. After all, in a fair world, only good things happen to nice people because they *deserve* to be happy. If life were fair, bad things would happen only to bad people, because they *deserve* problems and unhappiness. So if people are mean to you, or rejecting or abandoning, it must be because you deserve it, right?

But the truth is that bad things *do* happen to nice people, even nice people like you. If you continue to believe that life is fair and that niceness should protect you from bad things, you are setting yourself up for an avalanche of feelings of guilt when bad things happen to you, as they inevitably will. Because you tend to turn your anger inward, you will likely experience a great deal of depression as well.

Where Do Our Ideas about Fairness Come From?

Women are expected to be fair, patient, and tolerant. This is part of our biological and cultural heritage. As the primary caretakers of children, women usually do possess the inherent qualities of compassion, tolerance, patience, unconditional love, and forgiveness. But women tend to take these qualities to the extreme when it comes to their adult relationships.

Women often have a strong need to be fair or for things to be fair. They have a tendency to want to look at both sides of a situation. This need for fairness often prevents women from taking a stand on important issues and sets them up to be easily manipulated.

"My parents always told me to play by the rules. They told me that if I was a 'good girl' everything would work out for me. But that's not the way things turned out. I did everything right and I still got screwed." These are the words of a woman who had been emotionally abused for years by a man who was an expert at using her need for fairness to manipulate her. Each time she tried to stand up to him concerning his abusive behavior, he managed to turn things around on her by saying something like, "So, you've never done this before yourself, right?" Or, "You raised your voice at me last week; how can you criticize me for yelling at you?" (Of course, he didn't make the distinction that she raised her voice at him because he had been berating and belittling her for hours.)

Teaching girls that they need to be fair, understanding, and kind no matter what is a disservice to them. As one twelve-year-old girl told the author Rachel Simmons, "Teachers tell us that we have to respect each other and treat other people how you want to be treated. But that's not how it works out. People can be mean. Am I supposed to be nice to them even when they are mean?"

Another reason some women are overly fair and understanding is that they are working hard not to be like others who have been unfair to them. This was the case with Briana. "When I was a kid, my mother was extremely unfair to me. She would tell me to do something like water the yard, and I would go outside to do as she asked. Then she'd come out and yell at me for letting water flow onto the street. 'You're wasting water,' she'd shout at me, often loud enough for the neighbors to hear. I'd try to explain that I couldn't help it, that we lived on a hill and the water flowed downhill. But she wouldn't listen. She never listened to me when I tried to explain why I did something. She always just assumed that I was a screw-up. I'd get so angry with her. I remember telling myself that when I grew up I was never going to be unfair to my kids like that."

The problem was that Briana took her need to be fair to extremes. Whenever someone messed up in some way—whether it was a friend, a co-worker, or a boyfriend, Briana always gave the person the benefit of the doubt. This might seem to be a good quality but, in reality, it set up Briana to be taken advantage of. For example, Cindy, a good friend of Briana's, borrowed money from her over a year ago. Each time Briana asked Cindy to pay her back, she had some excuse: she didn't have any money because she got in a car accident and had to pay for the deductible, she needed all her money for books for school, she got a smaller paycheck because she was out sick. When I asked Briana if she believed all the excuses, she said, "I'm not sure. But I don't want to be unfair to her. What if she is telling the truth?"

Briana was even more extreme in her need to be fair when it came to her boyfriend, Jared. She and Jared had been seeing each other for two years and they had promised to be faithful to each other. But Briana kept hearing from her friends that Jared was cheating on her. "I refused to believe the rumors. Jared told me he wasn't cheating and I believed him," she told me firmly. Briana's faith in Jared was really tested when she found a pair of girl's underwear in his bed. "I was devastated. It seemed like my friends had been right all along," Briana said. "But Jared explained that he and his friend Kyle had gone out the night before, and Kyle had hooked up with a girl. He couldn't take her home, so Jared let them stay in his room and he slept on the couch."

I looked straight into Briana's eyes and asked if she really believed Jared. "Oh, yeah, that seemed like something he'd do." Eventually Briana could no longer give Jared the benefit of the doubt. She walked in on him while he was having sex with another girl.

Briana hadn't been feeling well, so she skipped her last class and came over to see Jared. She had his key and thought she'd surprise him. She did. Briana was devastated. She cried for weeks and eventually started therapy because she couldn't get over the fact that she'd been so naive. She couldn't stop thinking about all the girls Jared had probably been with while he was involved with her.

"I feel so betrayed and I feel so stupid. How could I have let this go on for so long? I was so sure I was right—that Jared would never cheat on me. I don't know if I'll ever trust anyone again."

Briana had gone so overboard in her attempts to be fair that she had been taken advantage of by her friends and her boyfriend. Don't let this be you. The following remedies will help you let go of your need for fairness and to stop believing that being nice will protect you.

Remedies

Remedy #1: Stop Your Magical Thinking

Believing in the protective power of niceness and fairness are holdovers from childhood. The truth is, we will not be spared loss, failure, or sorrow, no matter how good or fair we are. Life doesn't distinguish between saints and sinners when it dishes out tragedies and disasters.

The time for magical thinking is over. It is time to grow up. I understand that it may sound ludicrous for me to say this since most of you reading this book are already adults. But being an adult *physically* is different from being an adult *emotionally* and, unfortunately, many Nice Girls still have some work to do in that regard. A good place to start is by letting go of some of your most cherished assumptions, namely: "If I play by my parents' rules, if I do everything right, and work really hard to be nice, bad things won't happen to me," and "If I am nice and fair to other people they will be nice and fair to me."

To become a bona fide adult, you need to disentangle yourself from the web of illusions that provided you a sense of false comfort and protection when you were a child. The false assumptions that "life is fair" and that "bad things only happen to bad people" interfere with a deeper connection with your authentic self.

Exercise: Life Is Not Fair

The following exercise will help you to counter the sometimes powerful false belief that life is supposed to be fair.

1. Make a list of the most unfair things that have happened to you.

2. Read over your list. Notice if you come up with rationalizations as to why these unfair things happened (for example, "I learned a big lesson because of it," "I deserved it because I _____.").

3. Now go back over your list and say out loud, "It's not fair!" regarding each of the items on the list.

4. Go one step further and say out loud, "It's not fair and I hate it that this happened!"

Remedy #2: Stop Thinking in Black-and-White Terms

If you are like Briana, you need to not only face the fact that life isn't fair but to stop thinking in black-and-white terms. Because Briana's mother had been so unfair to her, Briana went overboard in her attempts to be fair. Being overly fair is just as much an extreme as being unfair and can be just as damaging to ourselves as being unfair to others is to them. Briana needed to learn that she could be fairer than her mother had been by being willing to listen to other people's excuses, perceptions, and realities. But that didn't mean she had to believe their perceptions or accept their excuses. She needed to connect with her own instincts and trust her own feelings to determine whether she believed someone and felt their excuse was valid.

This was difficult for Briana at first. Because her mother never believed her excuses, she continued to feel that she was being unfair when she questioned or discounted the excuses of others. But soon she was able to make the important distinction—she was, in fact, giving other people a chance when she listened to their excuses, unlike her mother. She learned that giving people a chance is not the same as giving them carte blanche. She still had a right to her feelings of hurt or disappointment, and she had a right to protect herself from being hurt in the future.

Briana told me at our last session, "It was always so important for me to be fair to other people but, ironically, I wasn't being fair to myself! Now I can be both. I listen to other people's excuses or explanations, but I also listen to my own intuition. If something doesn't sound right, I tell myself, 'I've got to listen to myself just like I listened to them.' And what I'm finding is that my intuition is right on. Now I don't get suckered by other people anymore."

If you identify with Briana, I suggest you do the following:

- When someone gives you an excuse for why he or she did something that hurt your feelings, disappointed you, or made you angry, remember that you can accept the excuse and still have your feelings about the offense, oversight, or omission.

- Say something to the person like, "I understand that you feel you had a good reason for [being late, forgetting to meet you or pick you up], but I want you to know that what you did hurt my feelings [or made me angry]."

- You can also take care of yourself by making sure the other person understands that you expect him or her to avoid making the same mistake again. You can say something like, "I'll let you off the hook this time, but please don't do this again" or "I forgive you this time but I don't want it to ever happen again. If it does, I won't be so understanding."

You can be fair and still be strong. You are being fair when you listen openly to other people's excuses or their side of the story. You don't have to do any more than that to be fair. You certainly don't need to accept their excuses or put yourself in the position of being hurt or disappointed in those individuals time after time. Giving people the benefit of the doubt doesn't mean you let them walk all over you.

Remedy #3: Create a Positive and Powerful Statement

Modifying your assumption that life is fair will go a long way toward helping you to grow up. Refer to chapter 4 for instructions on how to create a positive and powerful statement to replace the false belief that "being nice to others will guarantee that they will be nice to you" or that "life is fair."

Remedy #4: Replace Magical Thinking with Self-Soothing

Instead of relying on magical thinking to provide you comfort, start relying on yourself to give yourself the reassurance you need—not based on illusion but on the reassurance of reality. You can begin to soothe yourself with words of encouragement, as we discussed in the previous chapter.

6

Stop Worrying about What Other People Think of You

What other people think about me is
none of my business.

—SANDRA RAY

False belief: What other people think of me is more important than almost anything else—including my self-esteem, my health, or even my safety.

Empowering belief: It is far more important to know myself and take care of myself than it is to look good to others.

*This chapter is especially beneficial for
Prudes*

Nice Girls want everyone to like them. They want this even when they do not like the other person. "It's funny, really. I get so upset if I find out that someone doesn't like me. But often, if the truth be told, I don't like that person, either." This is what my client Amber told me when we began our work together. Why was it so important that people like her? As I got to know Amber, some possible answers emerged. First of all, her mother always worried about what other people thought of her. Also, she stressed to Amber the importance of being liked by others.

However, the primary reason Amber wanted everyone to like

her was that she had some abandonment issues. When she was twelve years old, a very vulnerable time for a girl, her parents got divorced. Instead of staying with her mother and seeing her father on weekends, which would have been the typical arrangement, she ended up living with her father. Amber's mother and father thought it was better if she stayed with her dad in the same house, in the same neighborhood that she grew up in. When Amber cried and begged her mother to let her come live with her, her mother explained that she needed time alone to "find herself." Besides, her mother tried to explain, she wouldn't be able to take care of Amber because she had to go to work. This didn't make any sense to Amber since her father had to go to work, too. Amber felt horribly abandoned by her mother, who she believed had stopped loving her.

Following the divorce, Amber's friends became overly important to her. Now, whenever someone doesn't like her, it triggers Amber's feelings of abandonment.

My client Leslie also had a need for everyone to like her. This extended even to her ex-husbands. "Even though we are divorced, I want everything to be nice between us," Leslie explained. When I asked her why this is, she started to cry. "I don't know exactly. If someone is not thinking well of me, I feel horrible. I go out of my way to be nice to them so they will like me again."

The major problem for Leslie was that both her ex-husbands were emotionally abusive, and she really needed to have as little contact with them as possible. The more contact she had with them, the more she doubted her perceptions. They were both able to twist the truth so much that Leslie ended up feeling confused and disoriented. But because of her need for their approval, she felt bad when she wasn't connected to them. She was in a real bind.

We needed to get to the source of Leslie's need for her ex-husbands' approval. As is often the case, the situation began in her childhood. Leslie was raised by a mother who liked girls and didn't like boys. "Girls were easier to control," Leslie told me. Because of this, Leslie and her sister got preferential treatment, while her two brothers were badly treated by her mother. This created a great deal of tension between the male and female siblings. Her brothers were older than she, and, when she was young, they picked on her relentlessly. But the worst treatment came when she was older. Her brothers either ignored her or showed obvious disdain for her. They made faces when she talked, argued with her when she stated her opinion, and talked negatively about her to others. "To this day, my oldest brother can't stand me," Leslie admitted to me. "His wife doesn't like me either, and I know it is because of things he's told her."

Because of this experience with her brothers, Leslie felt so uncomfortable and afraid when someone showed any sign of dislike or disapproval of her that she went out of her way to change the person's mind about her.

Women and Self-Image

In addition to childhood issues that set us up to worry too much about what others think of us, women in particular are socialized to worry about their appearance. A lot has been written about the current focus on body image. One of the main reasons so many women perceive their bodies negatively is that we live in a culture that dictates that women must be beautiful to be worthwhile and then sets up standards of female beauty that are not only impossible for most women to live up to, but are unhealthy as well. For example, many diets and all surgery to control weight are physically dangerous.

Getting and staying thin have become major pastimes for women, consuming a significant amount of our time, energy, and money. The entertainment and advertising media not only promote certain ideals concerning our appearance but often, in the absence of other sources of information, teach us untruths about what a normal and healthy body should look like. By trying to conform to our culture's ridiculous ideas, we place ourselves in a no-win situation in which we will never be satisfied with our bodies.

Ellie was constantly worried about what other people thought of how she looks. She always wanted to make a good impression, so she spent a lot of time on her wardrobe, her makeup, and her hair. "It's almost a full-time job making myself look beautiful," she shared during a luncheon with a group of women. "You won't believe what I went through to get ready for today," she added with a laugh. Several of the other women nodded in agreement.

This particular group of women was from Atlanta, Georgia, where I was attending a conference. The subject of how Southern women worry about their public image came up. "I think Southern women worry more than most people about what others think about them," one woman volunteered. "Our mothers drum it into our heads that we need to be concerned about our reputation. It's like we live our lives in the public spotlight—and we aren't even movie stars!"

Many of the women in the group agreed and told stories about how their mothers had stressed the importance of looking good to the public. One woman recalled that her mother had repeatedly told her, "You just can't afford to give anyone the opportunity to bad-mouth you."

While women in the South may have an extreme version of worrying about their public image, they are not unique in this regard. Most people are concerned about their appearance; however, women tend to focus on "what other people think" a lot more than do most men. Some of this is due to the amount of importance put on girls and women to be feminine or ladylike. As mentioned earlier, to attain the culturally prescribed feminine ideal, girls are taught early on to appear to be nice, pretty, and selfless and to hide their true selves if it conflicts with what is expected in their peer environment.

How Our Public Image Is Created

Our public image is created when we learn as children that there is acceptable and unacceptable behavior. Our parents and other authority figures socialize us by rewarding the former and punishing the latter. Unfortunately, this can lead us to believe that others will not like us if we are ourselves and that we must suppress (ignore) or even repress (deny or "forget") the unacceptable parts of ourselves. Those who were raised in families where they were severely criticized, expected to be perfect, or physically or verbally abused are particularly susceptible to believing that they must be perfect to be acceptable.

This was my situation. Raised by an extremely critical, disapproving mother, I grew up believing I was acceptable only if I was a good girl—which meant always obeying my mother, never questioning authority, and always being polite and kind to others. When I was bad, my mother would verbally humiliate me—often in front of others. She would also stop speaking to me—sometimes for days at a time.

My mother's public image was extremely important to her (she had, incidentally, been raised in the South). Since I was an extension of her, my public image was important to her as well. That meant that no matter how I felt about people, I was supposed to be cordial to them and at least *pretend* that I liked them.

When I started dating, I continued my good-girl act. I assumed that the only way I could get men to like me was to passively and compliantly go along with whatever they wanted. I smiled sweetly, listened attentively, and was caring and generous—especially with myself—if you know what I mean.

Pretending

We all try to impress others. We all pretend to be someone we are not in order to gain the approval of others. Think about it: How many times have you pretended to like something when you really didn't or pretended that you agreed with someone when you didn't at all? How many times have you given the impression that you are more understanding or more accepting than you actually are?

What's the harm in doing these things? After all, everyone does it. It's all a part of being polite, of being social. The problem is that is creates a false impression so that the other person doesn't really know you. It can even set a precedent for you to be expected to continue to put up with behavior you find boring or unacceptable. The most dangerous part of pretending is that, over time, if you pretend enough, you may lose touch with how you really feel, what you really believe, even who you really are—you begin to disappear. The real you begins to fade away behind the shadow of your facade.

Interestingly, it is often women who do most of the pretending. Since women are innately more compassionate, they often pretend so as to protect the feelings of others. In addition, girls are trained to be more agreeable and diplomatic than boys.

This pretending is just another way of lying, as Alice Koller, in her wonderful book *An Unknown Woman: A Journey of Self-Discovery*, so poignantly states:

> But think of the ways there are to lie, and I'll have done every one of them. Pretending to like something because someone in authority does. Evading a question. Saying only part of what I believe. Not saying anything at all. Shaping my words to fit what I know will be acceptable. Smiling when someone intends to be funny. Looking serious when my thoughts are

elsewhere. Agreeing when I haven't even thought over the matter. Drawing someone out just because I know he wants to talk. Trying to amuse in order to avoid talking about something I'm not sure of.

If People Get to Know the Real Me, They Won't Like Me

Everyone wants to be loved for who he or she really is. This is a deep and abiding human need. Unfortunately, many Nice Girls believe that if they are completely honest about who they are or if people really get to know them, others won't like them. Some even believe they are basically unlovable. This is especially true for women who were emotionally, physically, or sexually abused as children.

My client Lea had this belief. "All my life I found that people didn't like me after they got to know me—the real me. Boyfriends always fell in love with me right away because I'm pretty and they thought I was sweet. But after we got more involved, I always became jealous and critical. Once they saw this, they stopped loving me.

"So I've learned to push all those feelings down. When I get jealous, I don't say anything. I just silently steam. And when I feel critical, I stuff it and pretend that everything is okay. The only problem is that I usually end up falling out of love with the man. Now I'm the one who leaves."

Lea was no longer being rejected when she showed people her entire self, but because she wasn't allowing herself to be real, she couldn't maintain intimacy. Also, she was so convinced that she would be abandoned if anyone was to get to know the real Lea that she abandoned people first.

When What Other People Think Becomes More Important than Your Safety

Gwen, whom you met in chapter 1, was the woman whose boyfriend, Aaron, often treated her with disrespect after he'd had a few drinks. He'd grab her breasts in front of other people, brag to other men about what a "babe" she was, and urge her to dance with other men. You'd think that Gwen would get angry and leave whenever

Aaron acted like this, but instead she just silently put up with it. "I didn't want to cause a scene," she explained to me. "If I said anything to him, I knew it would just start an argument. And if I just left, how would that look to everyone?"

Gwen was far more concerned about people's opinions or about creating a scene than she was about her own feelings or even her self-respect. Worse yet, she cared more about what other people (including Aaron) thought than she cared about her own safety. The reason Gwen finally came to see me was not because of Aaron's behavior or even about her inability to stand up for herself. It was because one night when she was at a club with Aaron, she was raped.

As usual, Aaron had been drinking too much and, as usual, he started grabbing her breasts and buttocks, even when they were on the dance floor. Gwen tried to stop him by telling him she didn't like it, but he just laughed. When they finally sat down to rest, a man came over and asked Aaron if he could dance with Gwen. Aaron beamed with pride and said, "Sure, man, go for it. She's hot, isn't she?"

Gwen didn't want to dance with the man, but she didn't want to embarrass him, so she agreed. During the dance, the man kept trying to pull her close to him, but Gwen pulled away. He even tried to grab her buttocks. She couldn't wait for the dance to be over.

As soon as the music stopped, Gwen excused herself to go to the ladies' room. She didn't really have to go; she just needed a break from Aaron's obnoxious behavior and from the ogling eyes of the men around her.

When she came out of the bathroom, the man she had been dancing with grabbed her, put his hand over her mouth, and forced her down a dark hall. He was a big man and Gwen couldn't get away from him (she'd also had quite a bit to drink). With one hand still over her mouth, he pulled her panties down and forced himself into her. The music was blaring, and it drowned out Gwen's muffled calls for help. Within a few minutes, the man was gone.

Gwen crumpled into a ball and cried hysterically for several minutes. Then she went into the bathroom and cleaned herself up. After she had composed herself, she went over to the table where Aaron was drinking and quietly told him she wanted to go home. At first he resisted, but when he saw her face he knew that something was wrong. Again, Gwen didn't want to create a scene by telling him about the rape while they were at the club. "I knew he'd become furious and start yelling and then everyone would know what had happened to me. I just couldn't take that," Gwen explained.

She waited until they were home to tell Aaron what had happened. He threatened to go back to the club and find the man, but Gwen begged him to stay with her because she was so afraid. He finally listened to her and stayed. He wanted to call the police, but as she explained, "I was finally able to talk him out of it. I just felt so embarrassed. I didn't want to talk about it with anyone. I just wanted it to all go away."

Gwen came to me because she knew she needed help to recover from the rape. It had been several months, and she was still having nightmares. She couldn't have sex with Aaron, who was beginning to run out of patience. Yet she didn't have a clue that she had another problem—that her fear of "causing a scene" may have endangered her life and allowed her rapist to get away. I made it clear that it was not in any way Gwen's fault that she was raped. She may have been raped even if Aaron hadn't acted so inappropriately with her in front of other men. But I also explained that her overconcern with what other people thought of her had placed her in a dangerous situation.

Gwen was not alone in such overcompliance. It is not uncommon for women to put up with inappropriate or abusive behavior from boyfriends and spouses rather than "make a scene" in public or risk people's finding out that their relationship isn't working out. Instead, the women smile and act gracious and pretend the undesirable behavior doesn't bother them. It is also not uncommon for women to not report being date-raped, raped, or battered because they are embarrassed or do not want their own reputation tarnished.

If you identify with Gwen in any way, it is important for you to understand that this need to protect your public image at the cost of your self-esteem or safety is a blatant act of self-negligence and even self-destructiveness on your part.

Remedies

Remedy #1: Discover the Origin of Your Need for Everyone to Like You

In your journal, write about where you think your need for everyone to like you came from. Think about the messages you received from your family, authority figures, and society in general. Also, recall any childhood experiences that may have created this need.

Remedy #2: Learn That You Cannot Control What Others Think of You

This is a very important truth that we all must learn and constantly remind ourselves of. What other people think of us usually has very little to do with who we are. It has a lot more to do with the other individuals' issues—their prejudices, their fears, and projections. So it is a waste of time to constantly try to impress or please others.

Leslie, from earlier in the chapter, needed to learn this. As we continued to work together, she began to understand emotionally, not just intellectually, that what her brothers thought and perhaps still think of her had absolutely nothing to do with who she is. Once this understanding sank in, she stopped taking it personally when they showed their obvious disapproval of her. She realized that she had done nothing to cause them to think badly of her. And she also came to realize that being nice to her brothers wasn't going to change their opinion of her.

She also understood that she was repeating a pattern when it came to her ex-husbands. She was reacting to them the same way she reacted to her brothers—being nice to them so they would like her. "I realize now how ridiculous it all was. I don't even *like* my ex-husbands. They both treated me horribly. Now that I understand why I needed them to like me so much, they don't have any more power over me. I don't want anything to do with them."

We simply can't anticipate how someone will react to us. One person may like the way we look and act because we are a reminder of his or her mother, and another person may dislike us for the very same reason. That's why the quotation at the beginning of this chapter is so powerful—"What other people think of me is none of my business"—as is another popular quote: "You can't please all of the people all of the time."

Remedy #3: Create a Positive and Powerful Statement

Here are three suggestions for a positive and powerful statement to counter the false beliefs "I can control what other people think of me" and "What other people think of me is more important than almost anything else."

> Positive and powerful: Sometimes people won't like me, and it's okay.

> Positive and powerful: I like me, and that's all that matters.

> Positive and powerful: It's more important what I think of me than what someone else thinks of me.

Pick the one that resonates with you or create another one that feels better for you. Remember to repeat this several times a day—with feeling!

Remedy #4: Stop Pretending

We all want to put our best foot forward when we meet someone. But if you want to have healthier relationships in which your needs and opinions are respected and you are accepted for your true self, you will need to put aside your public self and risk exposing your true self. Instead of trying to impress people, you will need to show them all of you, including your not-so-positive qualities.

Being yourself can be painful at first. Even though you may have a strong drive to be seen as perfect, the truth is that we are all flawed human beings. Accepting that your imperfections and so-called negative attributes are part of what makes you unique will help you to stop continually trying to be someone or something that you are not.

Here are some of the benefits of telling the truth about who you really are. Read over the list now and return to it frequently as a reminder.

1. By telling the truth about who you are, you will attract those who genuinely like and appreciate the *real* you, not those who are merely impressed by a facade. This will make it more possible for you to find people you are truly compatible with.

2. Forming truer friendships, in turn, will help raise your self-esteem, since being accepted and appreciated for who you really are will make you feel more accepting and appreciative of yourself.

3. By exposing your true self, you are likely to discourage those

partners who are looking for someone they can manipulate or control or men who are looking for the perfect woman.

4. Most important, by taking the risk of telling the truth about who you are, you'll find that you feel stronger and more self-assured. In essence, by exposing your true self, you also create a stronger self.

Remedy #5: Risk Exposing Your True Self

It can feel frightening to risk exposing your true self. Your old, false persona has no doubt served you well in many ways. But it has also kept you stuck in the Nice Girl syndrome and sapped you of your power. The following example illustrates some of the other problems that come from your not being your true self.

Megan is a very charming person. It's hard not to like her. She just oozes a sweetness that is very appealing. You can't imagine that she could have a petty or angry thought in her head.

But underneath all this sweetness and light is a very resentful person. After working with Megan for quite a while, I discovered that she resents the fact that her life has been so hard. It seems to her that others have it far easier than she does: "When I look around me, everyone has more than I do. I have to watch every penny I spend, while my friends can go out shopping and buy whatever they want. It's hard not to be bitter. Sometimes I just hate my friends, because they have so much more than me."

So why is there such a discrepancy between how Megan really feels and how she acts? She learned very early on that if she were honest about how she felt, she would be criticized and even ostracized by her family. In Megan's family, it wasn't acceptable to complain. "If I complained about something, my mother would tell me to stop whining. If I continued, she'd punish me. One time, I complained that my food was too spicy, and my mother responded by saying, 'Okay, if you don't like it, go to your room.' I ended up going to bed on an empty stomach. Believe me, I thought twice about complaining about food again—or anything else, for that matter."

So Megan learned to keep her complaints to herself. She learned to hide any negative feelings and took on the cheerful and sweet persona that has served her well for many years—or at least she thought.

But Megan got into one abusive relationship after another with men. And she began to gain weight.

By the time she came to see me, her extra weight had begun to threaten her health. "I've got to lose weight. I can hardly walk, my knees are so bad, and I'm constantly in pain from my gallstones. But I just can't seem to stick to a diet."

It soon became apparent that Megan stuffed her feelings down with food. "It's been something I've done since I was a kid. Whenever I feel sad or lonely or angry, I eat to make myself feel better."

Megan and I set out to help her start expressing some of the feelings she typically stuffed down. I suggested she begin with small risks at first, such as opening up more with close women friends. I suggest you do the same.

Remedy #6: Shed Your False Self and Claim Your True Self

To discover your true identity, you will need to peel away your false self—that self you created to become socially acceptable. This is not the self you constructed to ensure your survival as a child, nor the facade you adopted to be loved. It is not the woman who made other people the center of her life, nor the woman who constantly tries to please others.

The effort it takes to sustain your false self is both draining and self-defeating. It requires much too much energy to continue to maintain it. Shedding your false self will involve risking other people's disappointment or even disapproval. It involves taking the risk of expressing your true thoughts and feelings, including those that are not socially acceptable or approved of in your family.

Underneath your public self and your false self, underneath your masks and facades, there is a core—your authentic self. Each of us travels through the journey of life with only one constant companion, and that is our true self. How sad would it be if your closest companion was someone you didn't even know? There is absolutely nothing as important as taking the time for self-discovery.

You can begin your journey toward self-discovery in a number of ways. The next three remedies outline the most effective ways—paths that women, including myself, have found to be most rewarding.

Remedy #7: Learning about Yourself through Your Emotions

The key to learning about yourself through your emotions is to experience them without inhibiting, judging, or distracting yourself from them. This practice is called being mindful. Instead of fighting your emotions or walling them off, being mindful of your emotions can help you discover more about who you are. The following steps will help you to experience your emotions in a mindful way:

1. Begin by simply observing an emotion. Notice how it makes you feel. Notice what happens in your body as you feel the emotion.

2. Do not judge the emotion as good or bad.

3. Fully experience your emotion. Allow yourself to feel the emotion as a wave, coming and going. Try not to suppress the feelings or push the emotion away. On the other hand, don't hold onto the emotion or amplify it. Just let it pass through.

Remedy #8: Find Yourself through Solitude

You don't need to seclude yourself in a remote area or lock yourself up in your home for days at a time to experience solitude. You can begin by just spending fifteen minutes a day alone, without the distractions of television, telephone, the Internet, or the radio. Just follow these simple suggestions:

1. Go to a quiet place in your home or outside where you won't be disturbed. If there are others in the house, ask them to not disturb you or put a "Do not disturb" sign on your door. If you have small children who can't or won't respect your need for privacy, ask a friend to watch them for a little while. Unplug or turn off your phone.

2. Sit quietly or lie down. Take a few deep breaths until your body begins to relax. Notice if there is any tension in your body, and breathe into that area to relax it. Ask yourself why that particular part of your body is so tense.

3. Notice what comes into your mind. Do you start obsessing about what you have to do or about other people? If so, try

to clear your mind of these obsessions and focus instead on discovering how you are feeling. Are you feeling angry? Sad? Afraid? Guilty? Or are you feeling grateful? Happy? Secure or proud?

4. Continue to focus on your body and your feelings. Notice what comes up for you—any nervousness, sadness, fear. Just notice the feelings; you don't have to do anything about them. Take a deep breath and just allow the feelings to be.

It can be extremely difficult to focus this much attention on yourself and your feelings. Many people have a hard time spending even a few minutes focusing in this way. You may become agitated or find all kinds of ways to distract yourself from yourself.

Your time of solitude may at first bring you only anxiety, fear, and sadness. Some women find that as soon as they spend even a few minutes alone with themselves, they are overwhelmed with a great sadness and that they spend their time of solitude in tears. If this happens to you, don't be afraid and don't let this discourage you. Your tears are there for a reason. You may have been pushing them away for years in your attempts to be nice and sweet and cheerful. Although it can be painful to cry all the tears you've been storing up, it can also be extremely liberating and healing. Many women have reported feeling as if a heavy burden was lifted once they allowed themselves to cry. This is particularly true for those who had traumatic or painful childhoods; these women needed to mourn their losses, disappointments, and woundings.

Others become so anxious they simply can't keep still. They spend their time alone, pacing, trying to calm themselves long enough to connect with what they are actually feeling underneath the anxiety. This is especially true for those who don't ordinarily spend any time connecting with themselves and their feelings. It can also be caused by having to face one's aloneness in the world. If it becomes too difficult for you to sit still, try taking long walks, especially if you can find a secluded place to do so. Let your walks become a moving meditation, a time to clear your mind and connect with your emotions and your spirit.

So be prepared for tears, anxiety, fear—even rage. Don't be surprised if your mind races a mile a minute and you are unable to get in touch with anything at first. Be patient with yourself and with the process, and keep trying. Your efforts will soon be rewarded. Only by facing yourself, including your inner pain, can you achieve contemplation instead of boredom, wisdom instead of despair, and serenity instead of conflict.

Remedy #9: Find Yourself through Journaling

Journaling can be a powerful tool for self-discovery. Your journal can act as a silent companion that listens without judgment. It can reflect back to you aspects of yourself you have never been aware of. And as you begin to put your feelings and thoughts down on paper, you will find that you feel less alone in your solitude and that you are becoming your own loving companion.

Writing in your journal can help you stay focused and provide you with an outlet for self-expression. As you record your feelings, innermost thoughts, and dreams, you will discover more about yourself than you ever imagined possible. You will discover thoughts and feelings long buried, solutions and alternatives to problem situations, new ways of looking at life-long issues, and, most important— new ways of looking at yourself.

Your journal can also be a place where you allow yourself to be completely who you are—no facades, no pretense, no saying what you think others want you to say—just the truth. Being totally honest with yourself can be difficult, but without complete honesty it is not possible to develop a true sense of who you are. I suggest you make a commitment to yourself to write only the truth in your journal or start a "truth book" in which you tell only the truth.

If you are having difficulty getting started, try the following techniques:

- Try writing with your less dominant hand (the hand you don't usually use).

- Try stream-of-consciousness writing (writing whatever occurs to you without editing or stopping).

Both of these techniques will help you bypass your internal censors and discover feelings that are buried below the surface.

Remedy #10: Come to Believe That What You Think of You Is Far More Important than What Others Think of You

You care so much about what others think of you because you want their approval. In actuality, however, the most important source of approval is your own. Unfortunately, Nice Girls do not approve of themselves much. They tend to be self-critical and to set perfection-istic standards when it comes to evaluating themselves and their own behavior. Although they may give others too many chances, they don't give themselves enough.

Several years ago, a great deal was written and discussed about the importance of feeling gratitude for what one has. It is my belief that it is equally important to feel personal pride. Unfortunately, most of us have been taught that pride is a negative emotion ("Pride goest before the fall") and that it is akin to being conceited or ego-tistical. But pride can be a powerfully positive emotion, especially for those with low self-esteem, who are self-critical, or who are perfectionistic. Having pride in yourself and your accomplishments is the best way to counter feelings of guilt, shame, regret, or self-criticism.

EXERCISE: WHAT ARE YOU PROUD OF?

The following ideas will help you to focus on the emotion of pride and to begin to use pride as a way to give yourself encouragement, acknowledgment, and positive reinforcement.

- Each night, before you go to bed, review your day and think about what you feel proud of. You may include the fact that you read a few pages in this book. Or perhaps you feel proud that you were able to say no to someone today.

- Make a list of the things you feel proud of each day.

- Complete the following sentence as many times as you can think of a response: "I feel proud of myself because _____."

My mother always told me, "Your reputation is all you've got." But in actuality, there is something more important than reputation:

how we perceive ourselves. Other people may admire you, but if you don't like yourself, you won't be able to take in their admiration. They may judge you negatively; this can certainly hurt. But if you judge *yourself* negatively, the result will be far more damaging to your self-esteem. It will take time to redirect your focus from the outside to the inside, but in time and with a real commitment, you can do it. Believe me, the time and effort will be well worth it.

7

Stop Trying to Be Perfect

> I would rather be whole than good.
> —CARL JUNG

False belief: I need to be perfect to be accepted.

Empowering belief: I don't have to be perfect to be wonderful (or loved).

or

Everyone is both good and bad, including me.

*This chapter is especially beneficial for
Pretenders, Prudes, Enlightened Ones*

Nice Girls have a powerful need to be good and perfect. Again, this partly comes from our societal conditioning. Even those girls who managed to get through childhood without disowning important parts of themselves in their quest to be accepted are confronted with another test—adolescence. In her book *Making the Connection*, Carol Gilligan discussed how a dramatic change occurs in girls when they enter adolescence—they fall asleep to themselves: "Adolescence is a time of disconnection, sometimes of disassociation or repression in women's lives. Women tend to forget or cover over—what as girls they have experienced and known."

The self-confident, competent, talented, exuberant, outgoing girl in middle childhood vanishes as she judges herself against an impossible feminine ideal—to please others; to be selfless, nice, and pretty; and to make herself the object of someone else's life.

To attain the culturally prescribed ideal, a girl must stash away a great many parts of herself. She must silence parts of herself and stop speaking out. She must stop expressing her feelings. Instead, she must focus on trying to please others, especially those of the opposite sex.

Parental Messages

Sometimes the pattern of trying to be good enough or perfect comes from having a parent who is never pleased. Justine came into therapy because she was deeply depressed. She knew she needed to get away from her current boyfriend but seemed to be unable to do so. "All my friends tell me that Frank is no good for me. They tell me that they've seen me getting more and more depressed since I've been with him, and they're right. Frank is unwilling and unable to commit to me. He always tells me that if I would only do such and such, he could commit. But then I do what he's asked and it's still the same story. He'll have another reason why he can't commit: I need to lose weight. My kids need to be older. I need to quit my job and get another, better-paying one."

As I questioned Justine, I discovered that Frank was not the first man she had gotten involved with who had been impossible to please. This made me wonder whether Justine had a parent who was a perfectionist. When I asked her about it, she replied, "I spent my entire childhood and most of my young adulthood trying to please my father. But no matter how hard I tried, I just couldn't please him. He wanted me to become a nurse, and I became a nurse. He wanted me to have grandchildren for him and I did. But he is never happy. There is always something else I should have or could have done."

Justine did what many other women do—she became involved with men who were like a parent; in this case, her father. Time after time, Justine chose men who could never be pleased. "I don't know why I never noticed this before," she told me after I pointed out the pattern. "It's absolutely amazing to me that I picked men like my father without even realizing it."

Perfectionistic Parents

We've all heard of perfectionistic parents who push their children to excel in a particular sport, in academics, or in other endeavors. These children are given the powerful message (sometimes spoken, often unspoken) that they have value only if they perform to their parents' satisfaction. Oftentimes, this is because a parent is living through his or her child, trying to make up for his or her own lost dreams.

René also had a perfectionistic mother. When she was growing up, she was supposed to help her mother around the house, bring home all A's in school, learn the piano, and take dance lessons. Needless to say, this was a heavy burden for a child. She hardly ever had a minute to herself to just relax, and whenever she complained about being tired, her mother would roll her eyes and say, "You don't know how good you have it."

Over time, René found that she gained a lot of recognition from others by getting good grades and excelling in music and dance. What had begun as her mother's desire for her to be perfect turned into her own need for personal perfection.

Perfectionistic parents put great value on appearances, status, material possessions, and what other people will think. Many feel strongly that anything short of perfection is failure. They also tend to disdain flaws of any kind. This makes them especially critical of their children's appearance. "My mother was always concerned about the way I looked," my client Veronica told me. "She hated my teeth, which were crooked like my father's, so she taught me how to smile without showing my teeth. She couldn't wait until I was old enough to get braces, but even then she seemed to be embarrassed by the fact that I had to wear them."

Her mother's concern about Veronica's appearance made Veronica very self-conscious. "I thought I was a real ugly duckling," she confided. "I thought everyone had the same reaction to my teeth and my braces as my mother did—that they couldn't stand to look at me. Today, even though I have nice straight teeth, I still smile with my mouth closed and put my hand in front of my mouth a lot."

Instead of receiving encouragement and support from their parents, children of perfectionists often receive only criticism, demands, and sometimes ridicule. Consequently, they may grow up feeling inadequate, incapable, awkward, or inept. Since they receive little praise or constructive guidance, their self-esteem is usually very low, and they have little faith in their own abilities. They are often overwhelmed with anxiety whenever they have to perform in any way, and this sets them up for failure. In addition, those raised by perfectionistic parents often suffer from any or all of the following problems:

- A sense that they are valued for what they *do* instead of for who they *are* (*doing* versus *being*)
- A tendency to be self-critical and never be satisfied with themselves or their performance
- A tendency to doubt and second-guess themselves
- An inability to identify and express their emotions
- Compulsive behaviors (extreme dieting, overexercising, compulsive cleaning)
- Depression
- A tendency to be a Nice Girl

Hypercritical, Shaming Parents

Hypercritical and shaming parents send the same message to their children as perfectionistic parents do—that they are never good enough. Parents often deliberately shame their children into minding them without realizing the disruptive impact shame can have on a child's sense of self. Statements such as "You should be ashamed of yourself" or "Shame on you" are obvious examples. Yet these types of overtly shaming statements are actually easier for the child to defend against than are more subtle forms of shaming, such as contempt, humiliation, and public shaming.

There are many ways that parents shame their children. These include belittling, blaming, contempt, humiliation, and disabling expectations.

- *Belittling.* Comments such as "You're too old to want to be held" or "You're just a cry-baby" are horribly humiliating to a child. When a parent makes a negative comparison between his or her child and another, such as "Why can't you act like Jenny? See how she sits quietly while her mother is talking," it is not only humiliating but teaches a child to always compare himself or herself with peers and find himself or herself deficient by comparison.

- *Blaming.* When a child makes a mistake, such as breaking a vase while rough-housing, he or she needs to take responsibility. But many parents go way beyond teaching a lesson by blaming and berating the child: "You stupid idiot! Do you think money grows on trees? I don't have money to buy new vases!" The only thing this accomplishes is shaming the child to such an extent that he or she cannot find a way to walk away from the situation with his or her head held high.

- *Contempt.* Expressions of disgust or contempt communicate absolute rejection. The look of contempt (often a sneer or a raised upper lip), especially from someone who is significant to a child, can make him or her feel disgusting or offensive. When I was a child, my mother had an extremely negative attitude toward me. Much of the time she either looked at me with the kind of expectant expression that said, "What are you up to now?" or with a look of disapproval or disgust over what I had already done. These looks were extremely shaming to me, causing me to feel that there was something terribly wrong with me.

- *Humiliation.* There are many ways a parent can humiliate a child, such as making him or her wear clothes that have become dirty. But as Gershen Kaufman stated in his book *Shame: The Power of Caring,* "There is no more humiliating experience than to have another person who is clearly the stronger and more powerful take advantage of that power and give us a beating." I can personally attest to this. In addition to shaming me with her contemptuous looks, my mother often punished me by hitting me with the branch of a tree, and she often did this outside, in front of the neighbors. The humiliation I felt was like a deep wound to my soul.

- *Disabling expectations.* Parents who have an inordinate need to have their child excel at a particular activity or skill are likely to behave in ways that pressure the child to do more and more. According to Kaufman, when a child becomes aware of the real possibility of failing to meet parental expectations, he or she often experiences a binding self-consciousness. This self-consciousness—the painful watching of oneself—is very disabling. When something is expected of us in this way, attaining the goal is made harder, if not impossible.

Yet another way that parents induce shame in their children is by communicating to them that they are a disappointment to them. Such messages as "I can't believe you could do such a thing" or "I am deeply disappointed in you" accompanied by a disapproving tone of voice and facial expression can crush a child's spirit.

The Legacy of Shame

Since shame is so debilitating, it makes sense that we would do almost anything in our power to try to avoid it. Human beings strive to stay in control, partly because we are raised to believe that we are responsible for what happens to us and that we can control our own lives. When something goes wrong, we may feel ashamed about the fact that we have lost control. This is especially true of children who, instead of simply believing that something bad "just happened," usually believe that they somehow caused or contributed to the events and are therefore responsible.

If one or both of your parents was perfectionistic, hypercritical, or shaming, you will probably be perfectionistic as well. You'll expect yourself to do things right the first time, and when you make a mistake you will not be forgiving of yourself. Instead, you'll berate yourself with such comments as "What's wrong with you?" and "Stupid, you can't do anything right." Your self-chastisement may sometimes be brutal, causing you to become depressed or despondent when you make a mistake. Although others seem to be able to move on after making a mistake, you are inclined to dwell on it, and this continually damages your self-esteem and makes you try even harder to be a Nice Girl.

Another legacy of having been shamed as a child or having perfectionistic parents is to have a tendency to continually evaluate yourself, judge yourself harshly, and set unreasonable expectations and standards for yourself.

You may also become involved with partners and friends who are perfectionistic. In fact, it is very common for women who were raised by perfectionistic parents to become involved with partners who are perfectionists, as it was with Justine, whom you met earlier in the chapter.

Your Inner Critic

Your inner critic (also known as the superego or the judge) is a pervasive yet often invisible presence in your life. It speaks to you inside your head with harsh, critical words. A woman raised by nurturing, supportive parents normally develops a healthy inner critic who represents internalized rules and consequences. This healthy inner critic causes her to feel "signal anxiety" when contemplating an action that goes against her value system, and guilt and sometimes depression if she actually transgresses. In this way, a healthy inner critic provides self-imposed punishment that keeps the woman's behavior under the control of her system of morality. Anxiety, guilt, and depression are kept within reasonable bounds since her conscience is modeled on her parents' reasonable attitudes. We internalize the inner critic and its standards to keep our parents with us and to give ourselves a sense of protection, safety, and imagined power over ourselves and reality.

Everyone has this critical inner voice, but Nice Girls often have a more vicious and vocal one that attacks and judges them harshly. This less healthy inner critic probably treats you with the same lack of understanding and acceptance that you experienced from perfectionistic or critical parents (or other caretakers or authority figures) while you were growing up. This less healthy inner critic causes you to set unreachable ideals, which in turn causes you to keep trying to reach that perfect image, never letting you rest or feel satisfied. Its demands are never ending, and the actual feeling you are left with is, "I am not good enough, and I never will be."

If you are like most Nice Girls, your inner critic not only evaluates you according to its standards, it also constantly compares you with other people. For example, when you are doing well according to one standard, there is always someone who is doing better, with whom you can compare yourself. If you are different from someone in some way, this translates to you that one of you must be better than the other.

Our Shadow Self

Another concept related to perfectionism is the concept of the shadow, or our dark side. As we've seen, many women have worked hard all their lives to be "good." They've done everything that has been expected of them—they were dutiful daughters, good students, devoted wives, caring mothers, responsible career women. But behind the facade of the loving, selfless, kind, innocent girl often lies an angry, resentful, competitive, jealous, selfish woman who is tired of her good-girl act.

There is a part of ourselves that we hide away not only from others but from ourselves. All of our lives, we have banished unwanted aspects of our personality into what psychoanalyst Carl Jung called our "shadow"—those traits, characteristics, attitudes, experiences, fantasies, and feelings that have been repressed into the unconscious. All of these suppressed parts of us are clamoring to get out. Unfortunately, most women are afraid to allow them out in the open. Instead, they smile sweetly and try to be perfect. Or they become involved with bad boys who will act out their dark side for them.

Jung believed that what we are unwilling to face in ourselves, we will be forced to encounter in the world. What we can't tolerate or acknowledge in ourselves, we often project onto others. This is one explanation as to why Nice Girls often get involved with men who are dishonest, manipulative, angry, or abusive.

For example, let's say that you were raised by an authoritarian father who frightened you so much that you could never show your anger toward him. The very thought of expressing yourself may have been so threatening that you felt you must deny and repress any signs of anger to protect yourself from his wrath. Instead, you presented a face of submission, obedience, and pleasantness. This face is a false face, masking your true feelings. As time went by and you continued to mask your anger with pleasantness, the mask became thicker and your shadow became larger. In time, the process of falsifying your feelings became second nature and was totally unconscious.

Thus, anger became part of your shadow, and pleasantness became part of your persona. Since anger was not an acceptable emotion for you to express, you may have become attracted to a person who expresses his anger openly, perhaps even abusively. Or, you may have become involved with someone who has the same inner conflict you have about anger and who also puts on a false front to others but is secretly seething.

Our shadow usually begins to form early in childhood, when we learn from our parents and other authority figures that certain emotions and behaviors are unacceptable. To avoid punishment and gain approval, we learn to repress these emotions and avoid those behaviors. For example, whereas girls often learn that the expression of anger is unacceptable, boys often learn that crying is unacceptable. Thus, anger and assertiveness often becomes part of a girl's shadow, and vulnerability and weakness become part of a boy's.

Women in particular often hide their dark side behind a mask of sweetness, innocence, and fragility. But when you embrace this dark side and let go of your need to be good and perfect, you will be rewarded with more energy, power, spontaneity, creativity, and positive sexual feelings—often called our Golden Shadow. We'll look at ways to do this in the following section.

Remedies

Remedy #1: Rediscover and Reclaim Your True Self

Since many girls abandoned their true selves in adolescence so as to be accepted by others, Nice Girls often need to go through a process of rediscovering themselves and reclaiming who they really are.

You began this process in the previous chapter. Now you need to go back and recapture the self-confidence you felt before adolescence. You need to reclaim the outspokenness, enthusiasm, adventurousness, and vitality you once had as a young girl. You need to go back to following your own instincts. You need to find your true voice and rediscover your strengths. The following exercise will help you to begin this journey.

EXERCISE: WHAT YOU LEFT BEHIND

1. Sit quietly and take a few deep breaths. Remind yourself of what you used to do as a child for fun. Remember a talent or passion you had as a child (for example, dancing, painting, swimming). What happened to that talent or passion? Were you encouraged or discouraged from continuing it? Did you compare yourself with others and give up?

2. Now imagine yourself reclaiming this talent or passion. Actually see and feel yourself doing it again.

3. Notice if any negative thoughts emerge, such as "You shouldn't be wasting your time with this" or "People will laugh at you" or "You're too old to do this."

4. Tell these voices to shut up! Replace these critical voices with a nurturing voice that says something like "It doesn't matter what others think" or "It's okay to have fun."

5. Make a promise to yourself to bring that talent or passion back into your life—to again experience the joy and exhilaration you felt when you were swept up into it as a child.

Remedy #2: Stop Expecting Perfection from Yourself

Those who were shamed as a child often strive for perfection as a way to compensate for an underlying sense of defectiveness and to avoid being shamed in the future. The reasoning goes like this: "If I can become perfect, I am no longer vulnerable to being shamed." Unfortunately, the quest for perfection is doomed to fail, since no one can be perfect. Each time you fall short of perfection, you will probably reawaken the already-present sense of shame you were trying to run from in the first place. And if you expect perfection from yourself, you will constantly be disappointed in yourself and continuously be damaging your self-esteem.

If the above information describes you, the first thing you need to do is to begin shifting your focus away from your so-called faults and instead focus on your positives.

EXERCISE: GIVE YOURSELF CREDIT FOR YOUR POSITIVE ATTRIBUTES

1. List five of your most positive characteristics—those attributes that you feel best about and are most proud of. If you cannot think of five things, continue thinking about it and observing yourself until you can.

2. If you still cannot think of five positive attributes, ask a close friend to tell you what she values and admires most in you.

3. Write down these attributes on an index card and place it in a conspicuous place where you can look at it often (some people have placed the card on their car dashboards or on their mirrors at home). Stop to read your list at least twice a day. Begin by taking a deep breath. As you breath in, take in the knowledge that you possess this quality. Now acknowledge this positive attribute by saying it out loud.

4. Make it a practice to give yourself credit for the good things you have done or for the progress that you make. Tell yourself, "You did a good job" or "You're getting better at this."

Remedy #3: Create a Positive and Powerful Message

Following the instructions in chapter 4, create a positive and powerful statement to counter the message that you must be good and perfect. Useful examples might be: "I'm not perfect and that's okay," "I don't have to be perfect to be wonderful," and "I don't have to be perfect to be loved."

Remedy #4: Identify Your Inner Critic

The sad truth is that it doesn't matter what you have accomplished in life, how much success you experience, how beautiful you are, or what efforts you make to raise your self-esteem—if you have a powerful inner critic who chastises you constantly or who discounts your achievements at every turn, your self-esteem will always be low.

Your inner critic has many roles. It is that part of you who:

- Blames you for things that go wrong
- Calls you names such as "stupid," "ugly," and "weak" and makes you believe that the names are true
- Compares you to others—especially to their achievements and abilities—and finds you wanting
- Sets impossible standards of perfection
- Tells you to be the best and that if you are not the best, you are nothing
- Beats you up for the smallest mistake

- Keeps track of your failures or shortcomings but doesn't remind you of your accomplishments or strengths ﹦

- Exaggerates your weaknesses by telling you that you "*always* screw up a relationship," "*never* finish what you started," or "*always* say stupid things"

Your inner critic may be experienced consciously as a thought or a "voice," but most of us are unaware of its habitual activity. Usually we become aware of it only during stressful situations when our shame is activated. For example, when we make a mistake, we might hear an inner voice that says something like "What an idiot!" or "There you go again, can't you get anything right?" Before giving an important presentation at work or a speech in front of a class or group, we might hear, "You should have prepared more; you're going to make a fool of yourself" or "Everyone is going to see how nervous you are." My client Marianne described her inner critic in this way: "I have a voice inside my head that is relentless. All I hear is, 'You messed up,' 'You didn't do it good enough,' 'You're a failure.'"

Even when you do become aware of the internal attacks, they can seem reasonable and justified. The judging, critical inner voice seems natural, a familiar part of you. But with every negative judgment, your inner critic weakens you and tears down any good feelings you have about yourself.

Your inner critic often appears as your own voice, making it appear as if you are the one who has these notions about what is right, what is necessary, or what things mean. But make no mistake about it, the voice you hear is not yours. It belongs to someone who lives inside you, someone you've brought along with you on your life's journey.

By paying attention to your self-judgments, you will begin to realize that they were learned from others. These standards can actually run counter to what you yourself want, feel, or know to be true.

Remedy #5: Determine the Strength of Your Inner Critic

This is how my client Tiffany described her dilemma. She can't relax and enjoy her life because she has a powerful inner critic who dominates her every action.

"I'm an educated woman but I feel so incompetent and stupid most of the time. I constantly compare myself with other people and always end up feeling inferior in some way. I'm constantly amazed by how other people seem to be able to speak up and not worry about whether what they say is going to be negatively judged by others. Other people tell me that they are impressed with how much I know and what a good job I do, but I don't trust others' assessment of me. I always think they just feel sorry for me and are trying to build me up."

If you identify with some or all of Tiffany's feelings, you also have a powerful inner critic. The following questionnaire, taken from my book *Healing Your Emotional Self: A Powerful Program to Help You Raise Your Self Esteem, Quiet Your Inner Critic, and Overcome Your Shame*, will help you determine just how powerful your inner critic is.

QUESTIONNAIRE: DETERMINING THE STRENGTH OF YOUR INNER CRITIC

1. Do you spend a great deal of time evaluating your performance, your appearance, your abilities, or your past history?

2. Do you set very high standards for yourself?

3. Is it difficult to live up to the standards you use to judge yourself?

4. Do you give yourself little breathing room to make mistakes?

5. Is your underlying sense of self often determined by your beliefs of what is right and wrong?

6. Is your sense of self often determined by whether you have met your own or others' standards?

7. Do you spend a great deal of time worrying that you have done something wrong?

8. Are you continually plagued by critical messages inside your head, messages that you are unable to quiet?

9. Do you constantly compare yourself to others or to the success of others?

10. Are you often envious of others' successes or achievements?

If you answered yes to only a few of these questions, your inner critic is not very strong. If you answered in the affirmative to many of these questions, your life and your experience of life are being dominated by your inner critic.

Remedy #6: Talk Back to Your Inner Critic

Your expectation of perfection from yourself will not change as long as you are constantly being bombarded by the negative messages from your inner critic. One of the most powerful ways of quieting and countering your inner critic is to talk back to it—literally. Just as you (hopefully) would not allow a bully or a tyrant to relentlessly criticize you or put you down, you cannot allow your inner critic to continue to wear away at your self-esteem.

Most people are very uncomfortable with the idea of talking back to their inner critic. It may seem silly, and since your inner critic is usually created by your parents' messages to you, it may feel as if you are talking back to your parents. If you are still intimidated by your parents, this can be a frightening prospect indeed. If the idea of talking back to your critic scares you, start off slowly, doing it only when you feel particularly brave or strong.

The following words and phrases have proved to be particularly powerful in silencing an inner critic. Choose those that feel good to you, that empower you—that make you feel angry.

- Shut up!
- Stop it!
- This is poison. Stop it!
- Get off my back!
- This is garbage!
- These are lies.
- These are the same lies my mother told me.
- I don't believe you.

- No more put-downs.
- Go to hell!

Catch the critic just as it starts—before it is allowed to weaken you or do much damage. Internally scream at the critic so you can drown its voice out with your anger. Profanity is perfectly healthy and may empower you further. If you do this whenever you hear your critic's voice, you will find that its attacks will diminish in frequency.

Remedy #7: Replace Your Critical Voice with a More Positive, Nurturing Voice

Unfortunately, you cannot permanently quiet your inner critic's voice by challenging it or telling it to shut up. This helps at the time, but eventually the voice will return. What you need to do is replace the critical voice inside yourself with another voice—a nurturing inner voice. You need to replace the critic's negative messages with positive ones (you began to do this in remedy 1).

1. Begin by focusing on replacing your critic's voice with a positive awareness of your essential worth, as opposed to the idea that your worth depends on your behavior. This means that you begin to entertain the idea that you are already enough just the way you are. You do not need to achieve anything more to be of value.

2. Repeat these words to yourself several times a day, especially when you find that you are being critical of yourself: "I am enough just the way I am." You may not believe this when you first say it, but eventually the words will sound more and more true to you.

EXERCISE: CREATING A NURTURING INNER VOICE

The following exercise, based on the work of Laurel Mellin, will help you create a nurturing inner voice.

1. Take a deep breath and begin to go inside yourself.

2. You may become aware of feelings of anger, sadness, fear, or guilt, or you may feel a void inside. Tell yourself that whatever you find there, it is okay. Continue to focus inside.

3. If you notice a wall of thoughts, step over the wall and begin to sink into yourself more deeply.

4. Continue to focus inside and see if you can find even a beginning sense of connection with yourself.

5. Bring up a nurturing inner voice. This is not a harsh or critical voice nor is it an overly sweet, indulging voice. It is a warm, loving voice that cherishes you and accepts you for who you are. In time, this voice will become your own but for now, it can be any voice that meets your needs (for example, the voice of someone who has been kind to you, the voice you use when you talk to a baby or a beloved pet).

Remedy #8: Develop Compassion and Self-Acceptance for Yourself

Compassion is the most powerful antidote to the poison of your unhealthy inner critic. When you have compassion for yourself, you understand yourself and accept yourself the way you are. You tend to see yourself as basically good. If you make a mistake, you forgive yourself. You have reasonable expectations of yourself and set attainable goals.

Compassion is a skill. That means that you can improve it if you already have it, or you can acquire it if you don't. The next time you hear your inner critic chastising you about something you did or did not do, counter this negativity by telling yourself something like "I'm doing the best I can" or "Given my circumstances, this is all I am capable of at this time." Learning to be compassionate toward yourself will also help you to raise your self-esteem.

Remedy #9: Don't Allow Other People to Demand Perfection from You

Women who were raised by perfectionists as well as those who are perfectionists themselves often attract partners who are perfectionistic abusers. Domestic violence usually starts with degrading behavior, insults, and put-downs. One partner begins to convince the other that he or she is causing unhappiness in the relationship and needs to change. Many Nice Girls believe that they must be the cause of the problems in the relationship and so they try harder to please.

If you are with a partner who is constantly complaining that you do not do enough or that what you do is wrong, you need to tell yourself that this person has a problem. He or she was more than likely raised by a critical, perfectionistic, or shaming parent, just like you were. But this does not give your partner the right to mistreat you the way he or she was mistreated. You also need to tell yourself that this person is never going to be pleased, so your attempts to please him or her are absolutely futile.

Remedy #10: Heal Your Shame (Especially Relevant for Those Who Were Abused, Neglected, Overly Criticized, or Shamed as a Child)

The following steps, taken from my book *Healing Your Emotional Self*, will guide you through the process of healing your shame.

1. *Accept the fact that you did not deserve the abuse or neglect.* Tell yourself that nothing you did as a child warranted any kind of abuse or neglect that you experienced. If you continue to blame yourself for your parents' inappropriate or inadequate behavior, you may need to get in touch with how vulnerable and innocent children are. Spend some time around children who were the age you were when you were neglected or abused. Notice how vulnerable and innocent they really are, no matter how mature they try to act. Ask yourself, Could these children ever do anything to warrant abuse?

2. *Tell your story.* As the saying goes, "We are only as sick as our secrets." By keeping the fact that you were abused or neglected as a child away from your close friends and family, you perpetuate the idea that you are keeping it secret because *you* did something wrong. Sharing your experience with someone you love and trust (your partner, a close friend, a therapist, members of a support group) will get rid of the secret and help get rid of your shame.

3. *Place responsibility where it belongs.* Although you may *intellectually* understand that the abuse or neglect was not your fault, you may not know it *emotionally*. You may still blame yourself. Absolutely nothing you did as a child warranted any kind of

neglect or emotional, physical, or sexual abuse that you experienced. You did not cry so much that your mother had to leave you all alone in your crib for hours at a time. You were not such a demanding child that your parents had to ignore you. You didn't have such a big head that your father had to "bring you down a notch or two" by telling you that you were stupid. Your parents' (or other abusers') reactions were their responsibility and theirs alone. It is vitally important that you understand this.

4. *Give back your parent's (or other abuser's) shame.* When an adult abuses a child, it is often because he or she is in the middle of a shame attack. He or she is, in essence, projecting his or her shame onto the child. While any form of abuse is taking place, the child often feels the shame of the abuser and is overwhelmed by it—causing the child to actually take on the shame of the abuser. You may have been told many times by your therapist, or by your friends and loved ones, that the abuse or neglect you endured was not your fault. Now is the time to start believing it. Releasing your anger toward your parents or other abusers will help you stop blaming yourself. The abuser is the appropriate target for your anger. Getting angry at your abusers will affirm your innocence.

5. *Allow yourself to be angry.* After several months of our working together, my client Mallory began to get more in touch with some of her anger toward her father for shaming her so much as a child. But this didn't sit well with Mallory, "I'm responsible for the good and bad about me—not my father. It's difficult for me to admit that I can be affected by anyone, much less him." Many people who were neglected or abused feel the same way as Mallory did. They prefer to take responsibility for how their lives turned out rather than to blame their parents. Holding your parents responsible for the way they neglected or abused you and the effects this kind of treatment had on your self-esteem is not the same as blaming. Blaming keeps you stuck in the problem, whereas righteous anger helps you move through the problem. Those who refuse to get angry at their abusive parents tend to sink into self-blame, shame, and depression. It is much healthier to allow yourself to release

your righteous anger than it is to turn that anger on yourself. By getting angry at your parents for their negative treatment, you are also more likely to be able to reject the negative messages that came along with that treatment—negative messages that still influence you today.

6. *Expect others to accept you as you are.* To heal your shame, you also need to consciously work on believing that it is okay to be who you are. This means you need to stop relying on anyone who treats you as if you are not okay the way you are. Surround yourself with people who like and accept you, as opposed to people who are critical, judgmental, perfectionistic, or otherwise shaming. Open up and deepen your relationships with supportive people. When someone treats you well, make sure you absorb it. When someone does something nice for you or says something nice about you, take a deep breath and soak up the good feelings. When you are alone, remember the positive or kind things the person said or did.

Justine, the woman who started therapy because her boyfriend refused to commit to her until she was "perfect," came to realize that the problem wasn't about her at all, it was about her boyfriend. "He's a perfectionist, just like my father," she announced to me one day.

After working on releasing her anger toward her father for never being pleased with her, Justine decided that she didn't want to be around anyone who didn't accept her exactly the way she was. "I'm just over it. Sure, I'm open to hearing someone's requests for me to stop doing something that really makes them unhappy, but if someone starts complaining about my behavior, I see it as a sign to get out of there. I just can't afford to be around critical people. I just won't do that to myself."

EXERCISE: GIVE THE SHAME BACK TO THOSE WHO HURT YOU

1. Sit comfortably and breathe deeply.

2. Imagine you are looking inside your body. Find any shame or bad feelings you might have there.

3. Imagine you are reaching down inside your body and pulling out all that dark, ugly stuff—all that shame and self-blame.

4. Now imagine you are throwing all that dark ugliness at the person who shamed you or abused you, where it belongs.

5. Open your eyes and make a throwing motion with your arms. Say out loud as you do it, "Take back your shame. It's not mine. It's yours." Do this until you can feel the truth of what you are saying.

Remedy #11: Own Your Dark Side or Shadow Personality

A major remedy for breaking out of the habit of trying to be good and perfect is to own your dark side or shadow personality. Owning your shadow does not mean pretending that the dark does not exist. Neither does it mean embracing the dark, as some practitioners of black magic or Satanism teach. What it does mean is that you work toward taking back all those forbidden thoughts, feelings, and undesirable and rejected personality traits. Only by finding and redeeming those wishes and traits that we chronically deny in ourselves can we move toward wholeness and healing.

Shadow-work forces us to take another point of view, to respond to life with our undeveloped traits and our instinctual sides, and to live what Carl Jung called the tension of the opposites—holding both good and evil, right and wrong, light and dark, in our own hearts.

The following shadow exercises will help you to identify and take back those aspects of yourself that were deemed inappropriate, unladylike, or bad.

EXERCISE: IDENTIFYING YOUR SHADOW

1. List all the qualities you do not like in other people (for example, conceit, selfishness, a short temper, greed, bad manners).

2. Take a look at your list and note which of these characteristics you find most offensive in others—those qualities that you not only dislike but despise, hate, or loathe. Circle these items.

The items you have circled form a fairly accurate picture of your own personal shadow. For example, if you circled greed as one of those traits that you simply cannot stand, and you tend to adamantly criticize others for this quality, you would do well to examine your own behavior to see if perhaps you, too, tend to be greedy.

Not all criticisms of others are projections of our own undesirable shadow traits. But whenever our response to another person involves excessive emotions or overreaction, we can be sure that something unconscious has been activated. If an individual is sometimes greedy, for example, there is a certain degree of reasonableness about your being offended by his or her behavior. But in true shadow projection, your condemnation of this person will far exceed his demonstration of the fault.

EXERCISE: ALLOWING YOURSELF TO BE BAD

1. Pay close attention to how often you monitor and censor yourself, how intently you focus on being good.

2. Try loosening the reins a little bit on yourself. If you are a workaholic, sneak out of work early or play hooky from work one day and go to the movies or some other fun activity. If you are a health fanatic, allow yourself one day a week to indulge by eating chocolate or some other delectable food. If you constantly monitor what you spend, ease up a bit and treat yourself to a new outfit or some other kind of treat once in a while. Most important, if you are always cheerful and sweet, even when you don't feel well, start telling people how you really feel.

You don't have to be perfect to be lovable. You don't have to be perfect to be wonderful, successful, and strong. So stop trying to be perfect and start accepting yourself—your flaws as well as your positive attributes, your dark side as well as your light side.

Turn down the volume of your inner critic and create a nurturing inner voice to take its place. When you make a mistake, forgive yourself, learn from it, and move on instead of obsessing about it. Equally important, don't allow anyone else to dwell on your mistakes or shortcomings or to expect perfection from you.

8

Stop Being Gullible and Naive

I tore myself away from the safe comfort of certainties
through my love for truth; and truth rewarded me.
—SIMONE DE BEAUVOIR

False belief: If I act innocent and naive, people will take care
of me and I won't have to grow up.

Empowering belief: It feels good to be a grown-up.

This chapter is especially beneficial for
Innocents, Enlightened Ones, Prudes

Dana is very childlike in her mannerisms. She often puts her
hand in front of her mouth when she giggles and she frequently
shrugs her shoulders when asked a question. Because she appears
to be so naive, people tend to take on a teacher role with her,
explaining how things work and solving problems for her. All this
works fairly well in helping Dana to avoid taking responsibility
for herself. But the price she pays is that the same people who help
her out also feel they have the right to order her around. She tends
to get into emotionally abusive relationships with men who are
controllers.

The reality is that Dana is still a child. She still wants someone
to take care of her. She plays helpless and dependent so that others
will take pity on her and come to her rescue. She refuses to grow up
and take responsibility for her own life.

Dana is also a dinosaur—a throwback to a more innocent time—a time when women routinely acted coy and naive as a way of getting attention from men and eliciting their protection, a time when men felt protective of women and enjoyed playing the white knight who came galloping to the rescue. But as mentioned earlier, women can no longer afford to play innocent or naive. There are no more white knights, and those who dress like them usually end up taking advantage of the women they rescue.

Pretending Can Be Dangerous

Women also can't afford to put their heads in the sand when it comes to the dangers all around them—everything from the threat of date rape and stranger rape to the ever-increasing practice of boys and men videotaping their sexual conquests and showing them to their friends. Neither can women continue to pretend that emotional or verbal abuse does not harm them or that a man who hits or shoves a woman once has never done it before and will never do it again.

Nina was constantly being manipulated and conned by other people. Her friends rolled their eyes and laughed when they talked about how many times she'd been talked into one scam after another. There was something very sad about just how gullible Nina really was. It's one thing to be the target of many scams, but Nina was also easily manipulated in her relationships with men. Time after time, she found herself becoming sexually involved with men she didn't even like.

This is what she shared with me when she finally realized she needed professional help and came in to see me. "My friends have been worried about me for a long time, but now I'm finally starting to worry myself. I realize that I just don't know how to take care of myself with guys. They are always able to talk me into sex—even when I don't want to. I always fall for their lines or I let my guard down, and before I know it, I'm having sex. It happens over and over, and I'm tired of it. I want to know what is wrong with me."

Nina told me story after story about how she had been manipulated by men. "I went out with this one guy who told me he needed to stop by his apartment to get something. Once we were there, he asked me if I wanted to see his apartment. I was curious about how his apartment looked—especially since I was thinking about moving soon myself. So I went upstairs with him. Once we got inside, he asked me if I wanted a drink. I didn't think anything of it and said, 'Sure.' We sat down on the couch to drink our wine, and before I knew it, he was kissing me. I liked the kiss but thought it was much too early in our relationship so I said, 'I think we better go.' Then he put his head down and looked really sheepish. He told me that he was really embarrassed because he'd recently lost his job and he didn't have enough money to take us out to eat as planned. He looked so pitiful sitting there that I felt sorry for him. I told him it was no problem—that we didn't have to go out to a fancy restaurant, that we could just order pizza.

"I thought the guy was going to cry. He told me that no girl had ever been so understanding—that I was an angel. He reached over to me and gave me a big hug. I could tell that he was relieved. He got up and ordered a pizza and then came back to the couch. We started kissing, and by the time the pizza got there, we were hot and heavy. He answered the door and got the pizza but came right back to me on the couch. I didn't want to be going so fast, but I really liked him. He seemed so nice, and I kind of felt sorry for him and I liked the way he kissed. We ended up having sex right there on the couch and eating the pizza afterward.

"I really liked this guy and I thought he really liked me. But he never called me again. To make things worse, I saw him about two weeks later at a really expensive restaurant with another girl. He didn't even acknowledge me when he saw me. I felt so used."

Nina had been used. And duped. Most women know the old, "I have to stop by my apartment" trick, but Nina seemed oblivious to this ploy. She not only ended up being a cheap date but had also gone against her own standards—namely, her promise to herself to never have sex on the first date.

Why was Nina so naive and gullible? Part of the answer was that her mother had been very naive, as I was to learn when I took Nina's history. Her mother was a stay-at-home mom who seldom ventured outside the home. "She always told us that her family was all she needed," Nina said. "She didn't even have many friends."

Nina's father seemed to like having her mother home. "They were a really traditional couple. Dad wanted his dinner ready when he got home, and Mom seemed to like waiting on him. 'Your father works hard,' she'd always tell us. 'You girls be quiet and let him relax.'"

When I asked Nina if her parents seemed to get along, she immediately responded with, "Oh, yeah. They really loved each other." When I asked if they ever fought, she once again answered quickly, "Oh, no. My mom never argued with my dad. She always agreed with everything he wanted to do."

Nina was painting a picture of a storybook family life—the dutiful wife, the hardworking husband, the kids who were seen but not heard. Or was it? Nina was a young woman who was raised in the eighties—not the fifties. Something just wasn't adding up.

After several more sessions and some gentle probing on my part, Nina finally opened up more about how it really was in her family. As it turned out, it wasn't so perfect after all. Yes, her mother was a dutiful wife, but her father was quite demanding. He expected his wife to wait on him hand and foot when he was home, and he was extremely hard to please. There were many nights when he refused to eat what she had cooked and insisted that she cook something else entirely. He complained if the house wasn't immaculate and the kids weren't bathed and dressed up when he got home. As we continued to explore Nina's childhood, Nina admitted that it really wasn't by choice that her mother didn't have any friends or didn't go out much. It was at her father's insistence that Nina's mother not associate with anyone outside of the family.

When I asked Nina how she felt with this new awareness, she said, "I feel sorry for my mother. I'd always thought she was happy just being our mother and my dad's wife, but now I wonder if that is true."

When I asked her how she felt about her dad, she made excuses for him. "I'm sure he had a rough life. He did work very hard, and I suppose he needed things to be just so in order for him to relax."

"And how do you feel about the fact that he basically isolated your mother? And about the fact that he was so controlling of her?" Nina avoided answering both these questions. She merely shrugged and looked away. I had expected as much. She had an investment in not facing the truth about her father. She had pretended all her life that her mother and father had a perfect relationship, and even though she was coming to see some of the chinks in her father's armor, she wasn't ready to completely come out of denial. This was at the core of Nina's tendency to be naive and gullible. As long as she pretended that there were no bad people in the world, that people didn't lie, cheat, or manipulate, she could continue to pretend that her father was a great man. But if she began facing the truth about people—that there are those who con other people, cheat other people, and control other people, she would open the door to seeing the truth in all its forms—including the truth about her father.

No More Mr. Nice Guy

Women are also naive and gullible in believing that a man who is being helpful to them is doing it just because he is a nice guy and not because he wants anything from them. While this can sometimes be the case, women cannot afford to *assume* this is true.

Jasmine first met Aaron at a dinner party at the home of one of her friends. Since he was much older than she was, Jasmine didn't think he was coming on to her but was just being friendly. He seemed very fatherly to her, offering her advice about everything, from how to find a better job to suggesting the best hotel at her favorite vacation spot. Before they parted that night, Aaron gave her his phone number. He said he knew the name of a headhunter who might be able to help her find a better job.

As luck would have it, the headhunter was able to get Jasmine a position at an incredible firm for much more money than she had been making. Feeling grateful to Aaron, Jasmine called to thank him. When he casually suggested they get together for lunch to celebrate, Jasmine agreed.

They had a wonderful lunch together. Aaron was a fantastic listener and Jasmine found that she could discuss almost anything with him, including her problems with her boyfriend. Aaron agreed with her when she told him that her boyfriend was inconsiderate and selfish. He told her that she deserved to be with a man who would make her the most important thing in his life. That sounded wonderful to Jasmine since her current boyfriend seemed to have difficulty making time for her. After lunch Aaron said, "Why don't you come with me this weekend to the premiere of . . ." (Aaron was in the movie industry in Hollywood). "It will cheer you up and it will send the message to your boyfriend that you aren't going to just wait around for him to call." Jasmine thought it was a great idea.

Aaron continued to help Jasmine in numerous ways and to listen to her problems regarding her boyfriend, with whom she eventually broke up. Ever so gradually, Jasmine came to depend on Aaron for advice and companionship, and eventually she began an affair with him.

As you read this example, you most likely knew where the story was going. You probably realized that all along Aaron was intending to become sexually involved with Jasmine. But interestingly, Jasmine did not know this. In fact, when I suggested it to her, she scoffed at the idea. "I really don't think you're right about that. I think he just wanted to be a friend to me . . . and a mentor. Our romantic and sexual feelings for each other just grew out of our friendship." Jasmine was being naive.

The truth is that it is very difficult for most men to put their sexual attraction for a woman in a box. They may try to be "just friends" with a woman they are attracted to and turn off their sexual feelings, but it usually doesn't work. Aaron likely decided that being Jasmine's friend was the way to get close to her, and he had hopes that it would turn into a sexual relationship. Because he was much older than she was, he probably realized he needed to use the "friend and mentor" card to get her to pay attention to him. Then once they became friends, he used the fact that he was successful to his advantage to impress her.

The extent of Jasmine's naïveté went even further. Even though Jasmine knew that Aaron was married and he was almost twice her age, she believed that they were meant to be together and that he would eventually leave his wife. Three years into the relationship, Jasmine sought counseling because she gradually came to the conclusion that she was just fooling herself.

It's Time to Come out of Denial

Still another way that women commonly play gullible and naive is in their refusal to accept that their partner and/or their children are capable of doing bad things. Some women continue to turn a blind eye to the misbehavior of their partners because coming out of denial would mean they would have to do something about their situation. I can't tell you how many women I've worked with who put up with inappropriate, abusive, or even illegal behavior from their partners because as soon as they admitted the truth to themselves, they would have to end the relationship.

My client Christina was a perfect example of this. Christina's husband owned his own business and had always worked long hours. But in the past three years, he had started working even longer hours, often not coming home until ten or eleven at night. He explained that he'd had a dinner meeting with a potential client. Christina told me that she didn't have any reason not to believe him; after all, he'd always been honest with her in the past. Then she started noticing that his shirts often had lipstick on them and smelled like perfume. She brought this up to her husband and he explained that sometimes his clients were women, and sometimes they hugged him when they said good-bye. "What do you want me to do?" he protested, "Push them away?"

These comments always made Christina feel silly. After all, her husband was an outgoing, friendly guy. Everyone loved him. It made sense that female clients would want to give him a hug to say good-bye. That was just the kind of guy he was.

Then Christina started getting phone calls in the evening and the person would hang up. This went on for about two months. Finally, one night she dialed *69 after the call, and a woman answered. Christina asked the woman if she had just called her house. The line went silent, and then the woman said, "Yes, I called." Christina asked who she was and why she had hung up. Again, there was silence for a few minutes before the woman said, "I was calling to talk to your husband." The woman said that she had had an affair with Christina's husband for about six months but that he had dumped her for another woman. She was angry with him and was calling to tell him off, but Christina was always the one to answer the phone.

Christina was horrified to hear this about her husband. Her first inclination was to tell herself that the woman was lying. Her husband had probably rejected her advances and she was doing this to be spiteful. She was probably just a stalker. But then Christina started to wonder if it could be true. After all, her husband was out late nearly every night, and he certainly had ample opportunities. Plus, she had smelled perfume on his shirts and found those lipstick stains. So Christina confronted her husband when he came home that night. He immediately became angry: "I can't believe she would call my home like that! What an asshole. I never touched that woman. She was always coming on to me, and I was just trying to be nice to let her down easy. I should have told her what I really thought about her. I told her I was married and to leave me alone. Boy, am I going to give her a piece of my mind!"

Then he focused his anger on Christina. "And how dare you believe her! Is that how much faith you have in me? Do you really think I'd break my marriage vows like that? What kind of a husband do you think I am?"

Christina felt about two feet tall. "I'm so sorry I doubted you," she said. "You're right. I shouldn't have listened to her. I don't even know her, but I was willing to take her word over yours."

Her husband remained angry for several days, even though Christina apologized many times. He finally started talking to her again and reluctantly told her he forgave her for doubting him.

She told me, "I can't believe that I apologized to *him* for doubting him. I had every right to question him. He turned the whole thing around and made me the bad guy when *he* was the one who was doing something wrong!" As it turned out, about two months later Christina was forced to finally face the truth about her husband when another woman called the house. This one didn't hang up but asked to speak to her. The caller told her that Christina's husband was in love with her. She thought Christina should let him go because they wanted to get married. Christina couldn't continue to remain naive about her husband any longer. The jig was up.

An experience like this can make a woman grow up fast. I'm happy to report that after several months of therapy, Christina did just that. First she allowed herself to grieve the loss of her husband and, equally important, to grieve the loss of her fantasy husband. Then she allowed herself to express her anger. Finally, she looked honestly at the reasons she had remained so naive. At our last session she told me, "I'm finally able to see people for who they really are—not as I want them to be. It's still painful sometimes. I still find myself wanting to pretend that people are all good and that they don't have any negative motives, but I catch myself in the act and come out of my fantasy. I'm not the naive person I was before my marriage and that gives me a sense of power and strength. Now I know I can face the truth about a person or a situation and still take care of myself." Brava, Christina.

Remedies

Remedy #1: Grow Up and Face the Truth

Childhood is a time for innocence. It is a time for fairy tales and magical thinking. But you are no longer a child, and the time for magical thinking and illusions is over. Although those illusions provided a sense of comfort and protection when you were a child, if you don't dismantle them you will remain a prisoner of childhood. You must give up the futile search for the security, trust, and unconditional love you longed for as a child. You must peel away the illusions that stand between you and reality.

Now is the time to face the truth about life—to create a shift in your thinking from magical to realistic. The truth is that no one is perfect—not even parents. The truth is that no one tells the truth all the time. People distort the truth, manipulate, and out-and-out lie to get what they want. We simply can't take people at face value. We must look under the surface. We must look for discrepancies, for exaggerations, for half-truths. This doesn't mean we need to become paranoid—just realistic.

You must come to realize that your unwillingness to face the truth about people and the world in general is putting you in danger. The danger may be that you will continually be fooled or conned by others or that you won't be able to recognize it when someone you love is cheating on you, or that you actually put your life in danger because you foolishly trust someone's word or naively trust that people are good. By facing these essential truths, you will be well on your way toward giving up your innocence, naïveté, and gullibility.

- You can't expect anyone else to take responsibility for your welfare. You are the only one who can take care of you.

- The price you pay for looking to someone else to take care of you is dependency, the loss of self, and, ultimately, the inability to control your own life.

- It is human to look out for our own self-interests. It is part of our survival instincts. This means that when a stranger approaches you and is nice to you—especially when that stranger is a man—you need to at least *consider* the possibility that he or she wants something from you—probably sex or money.

- Just because someone *seems* to be a nice person doesn't mean you can trust him or her. Con artists can be very charming people.

- Just because someone loves you doesn't mean that he or she is incapable of deceiving you or betraying you.

- It is *not* safe to overindulge in alcohol or to take drugs when you are out at a club or a party—even when you are with a group of friends. You *cannot* depend on your friends to protect you.

- Men are capable of controlling their sexual desires and feelings. Don't let any man convince you that he has "blue balls" or that he is physically harmed in any way because you won't have sex with him.

Remedy #2: Come Out of Denial

Like Nina, you may have an investment in avoiding the truth about your childhood. As long as you remain in denial about any painful or traumatic events that happened to you earlier in life, you will probably remain gullible and naive and thus risk continually being used, conned, or even abused by others.

For example, it can be quite painful to admit that you were abused or neglected as a child. You may experience tremendous pain as you remember how it felt to be treated as you were, and you may become extremely angry at those who abused or neglected you. You may feel a deep sense of loss as your idealized picture of your childhood or your positive image of a parent, another family member, or another adored caregiver is tarnished forever.

When you finally do face the truth about what happened to you as a child, you may become overwhelmed with sadness and anger. Allow yourself to feel these emotions. Don't try to fight them off. You've probably been doing that for too long. Allow your emotions to flow out of you. Cry for the little child who was mistreated in such terrible ways. Get angry at how the little child you once were was used or abused by adults who should have known better—adults who were supposed to protect you.

Unfortunately, most people who were neglected or abused box

off their pain and try to put it out of their mind. But this never really works. Experiences of neglect and abuse continue to wear you down emotionally, insidiously whittling away at your self-esteem.

Many people who were neglected or abused stay stuck in anger or in pain and never move through their feelings. Instead, they turn their feelings of anger on themselves and become depressed or riddled with unnecessary (and unhealthy) guilt and shame. Some punish themselves by being self-destructive (for example, smoking, driving too fast, provoking a fight with someone). Others numb themselves to their feelings and are unable to access their feelings of anger and pain from the past.

Emotions that go unexpressed often lie dormant inside us until someone or something reminds us of our past and triggers a memory—and the feeling. When this happens, we can become depressed and self-critical or lash out at those closest to us when our real target is someone from the past—someone we were likely afraid to express our emotions to at the time.

It can be frightening to lift the veil of denial. The scariest part is experiencing the intense feelings that lurk just below denial's surface. You may need professional help in dealing with all these strong emotions. For now, allow yourself to experience whatever it is that you are feeling and remember the following:

- Even though it may feel like it is happening in the present, it will help if you remind yourself that what you are feeling are memories of the feelings you had as a child. These things are not happening to you in the present. You have already survived your childhood and the painful things that happened to you.

- It helps if you breathe into an emotion. As it is with physical pain, if you breathe into the emotion, it tends to decrease and become less overwhelming.

- As powerful and overwhelming as emotions can be, they are actually positive forces intended to help you process an experience.

- As long as you don't allow yourself to become overwhelmed by them, your emotions will help you come out of and stay out of denial.

- Allowing yourself to feel and express your hidden emotions from the past will help heal you from the past.

EXERCISE: YOUR FEELINGS ABOUT
YOUR CHILDHOOD

1. Make a list of all the ways you were neglected or abused as a child.

2. For each item you have listed, write about the following:

   - How you felt at the time
   - The effect the neglect or abuse had on you at the time
   - How you feel now as you remember the experience
   - What effect you believe the experience has had on you long term—especially as it relates to your being a Nice Girl

3. As you write about each incident of neglect or abuse, allow yourself to feel whatever emotions come up for you. It is appropriate for you to feel angry, enraged, afraid, terrified, sad, grief-stricken, guilty, ashamed, or any other emotions you may feel. On the other hand, do not become alarmed if you do not feel anything. Survivors of childhood and neglect often numb themselves to their feelings as a self-protective mechanism.

4. If at all possible, share your writings with at least one other person. Most victims of childhood neglect or abuse did not have what is called a compassionate witness to their pain and anguish. Telling a loved one about what happened to you and receiving your loved one's support and kindness can be a major step in the healing process.

Now that you know the truth, it is yours to use for recovery. There is healing in discovering the truth, facing it, and finally in accepting it. Your realization of the facts about your childhood clears the way for dealing with your anger and resolving your relationships with your family. You have lived with lies, secrecy, and deception for a long time, and it has been painful. Learning to live with the truth will help free you from the pain and lead you toward a fuller, richer life.

Remedy #3: Begin to Face the Truth about the So-called Payoffs to Playing Gullible and Naive

Women who play gullible and naive generally do so because it pays off so well. One of the remedies is for women to begin to understand that the payoffs actually aren't as big as the price they pay in terms of their self-esteem, self-respect, and safety. They may get taken care of but they aren't respected. They may get special attention but from the wrong kind of people.

EXERCISE: PUTTING IT DOWN IN BLACK AND WHITE

1. Write down all the positives about acting innocent and naive—all the perks you receive from those behaviors.

2. Now write the negatives to acting innocent and naive.

3. Now compare your lists. If you are being honest, you should notice that there are many more negatives to playing innocent and naive than there are positives, or that the positives aren't as significant as the negatives you experience.

Remedy #4: Recognize the Payoffs to Growing Up

Women who play gullible and naive are usually trying to avoid growing up and taking responsibility for themselves. But there are many benefits to behaving in a more grown-up fashion. Recognizing these more substantial payoffs—such as gaining self-respect, the respect of others, and attracting emotionally healthier partners who do not need to dominate and control you—will help you to give up the payoffs you are now receiving.

EXERCISE: THE PAYOFFS TO GROWING UP

Make a list of the payoffs you can and will experience when you choose to grow up and take care of yourself.

Remedy #5: Create a Positive and Powerful Statement

Your naive and innocent act may be the result of your refusal to grow up or your desire to remain in denial. Whichever the case, create a positive and powerful statement to counter these negative desires.

9

Start Standing Up for Your Rights

> Remember, no one can make you feel inferior
> without your consent.
> —ELEANOR ROOSEVELT

False belief: I don't have the right to act on my own behalf.

Empowering belief: I have the right to act on my own behalf
when necessary, including saying no when I don't want to
do something.

*This chapter is especially beneficial for
Victims, Doormats*

There are many reasons women have difficulty standing up for themselves. They often find it hard to say no because they feel selfish if they refuse to help someone—even when their own needs are more important at the moment. In addition, they are often afraid people will dislike them if they aren't cooperative, as was the situation with my client Jayda: "No matter how obnoxious someone is, I try to get along with them. It's part of the whole thing about being 'nice.' I make sure I never alienate anyone, but in the process I get taken advantage of."

Women often have a fear that if they stand up for themselves, they will be seen as overbearing, domineering, or bitchy. Maria was raised to be obedient and polite. However, other people take advantage of her because of her niceness. She wants to start standing up for herself but doesn't know how to do it without feeling like she's being rude. "I hate it when women are aggressive. It is so unattractive. I want to stand up for myself but not at the expense of my femininity," she explained during a group therapy session for Nice Girls.

It takes a lot of courage and self-respect to act on your own behalf. It takes a strong belief that you deserve something better. Unfortunately, many women don't have this kind of self-respect and don't believe they deserve to be treated better. Many are afraid to hope for better treatment because they have yet to receive it. To be able to stand up for yourself, you need to give up waiting for someone else to come to rescue you and your belief that you have no power to change your circumstances. You will need to reach out—ever so tenuously—toward accepting that you have more power to change your circumstances than you think you do. Fortunately, when women focus their considerable strength and will to change something, they are often surprised at how much power they actually have.

You have the right to live your life the way you choose, as long as you are not stepping on someone else's rights. But rights don't mean much if you don't have the courage to claim them. Unfortunately, many women have had their courage stripped away by societal expectations and messages and overly domineering parents, or from having been emotionally, physically, or sexually abused in childhood or adulthood.

In this chapter, you will receive the information and encouragement you need to take the risk of standing up for yourself. You will be given the tools that will help you to find your courage and to begin to believe in yourself.

For some of you, claiming your rights will be the hardest thing you've ever done in your life.

Societal Reasons for Women's Difficulty in Standing Up for Themselves

Many women have learned to remain silent out of a sense of protection. As mentioned earlier, there is a long history of oppression against women, and we all carry this legacy inside us. Women are also silenced because of the misperception that we talk too much and how men treat us when we do try to stand up for ourselves.

Studies have documented that women actually speak less than men do and get interrupted more often. Also, women often find that when they do try to speak up, they are not taken seriously; they are ignored, undermined, or misunderstood. Research shows that men tend to not listen to women, even when the women are their bosses. Because of this, many women have learned to remain silent.

Unfortunately, as women, we need to learn that silence doesn't really protect us and that there is a price to pay for remaining silent. In fact, our silences not only do not afford us protection but render us more vulnerable. They label us as weak and wimpy. By remaining silent when someone offends us, crosses a boundary, or becomes abusive, we in essence give that person permission to continue his or her inappropriate behavior.

Childhood Experiences and the Fear of Standing Up

Women who experienced abuse in their childhood homes (either directly or vicariously—by witnessing their mother or another child being abused) are far more likely to have difficulty standing up for themselves than are women who did not experience abuse. For example, many battered women share the common characteristics of low self-esteem, a poor self-image, and a childhood marred by abuse or neglect. Women who were abused (either emotionally, physically, or sexually) or neglected by family members have little or no concept of normal family intimacy that they can bring to adult relationships. Being hurt by those who were supposed to love and protect them is nothing new.

According to the *Comprehensive Textbook of Psychiatry*, the common denominator of psychological trauma is a feeling of "intense fear, helplessness, loss of control, and threat of annihilation." Survivors of childhood abuse consistently report an overwhelming sense of helplessness. In abusive families, rules are usually erratic, inconsistent, or patently unfair, and survivors frequently report that what frightened them the most was the unpredictable nature of the violence. Unable to find any way to avert the abuse, they learn to adopt a position of complete surrender that they often carry into their adult lives and relationships.

The constant fear of death is reported by many survivors. Sometimes the child is silenced by violence or by a direct threat of murder. The man who molested me when I was nine threatened to kill me if I told anyone, and I believed him, since I knew he had already been in a mental hospital, supposedly for beating his ex-wife. More often, survivors report threats that resistance or disclosure will result in the death of someone else in the family. Threats of violence may also be directed against pets; many survivors report being forced to witness the sadistic abuse of animals.

Children in an abusive environment develop extraordinary abilities to scan for warning signs of attack. They become what is commonly referred to by professionals in the field as hyper-vigilant, meaning that they develop extraordinary abilities to notice any warning signs of an impending attack. They learn to recognize subtle changes in the facial expression, voice, and body language as signals of anger, sexual arousal, intoxication, or disso-ciation.

When abused children note signs of danger, they attempt to pro-tect themselves by either avoiding or placating the abuser. Some become quiet and immobile. The result is the peculiar, seething state of "frozen watchfulness" noted in abused children.

When avoidance fails, children attempt to appease their abusers through obedience. The arbitrary enforcement of rules, combined with the constant fear of serious harm or death, produces a paradox-ical result. On the one hand, it convinces children of their utter help-lessness and the futility of resistance. Many develop the belief that their abusers have absolute or even supernatural powers, can read their thoughts, can control their lives entirely. On the other hand, it motivates children to prove their loyalty and compliance. They dou-ble and redouble their efforts to gain control of the situation in the only way that seems possible—by trying to be good. It is easy to see how this learned helplessness and need to please can translate into a victim pattern in adulthood. We see the very same behaviors in battered women.

When I first met Teresa, I knew she had been terrorized in some way. She had the look of a deer caught in the headlights. She stared straight ahead and didn't blink her eyes, and her eyes also had the familiar glazed-over look that I have seen so often in abuse victims. She had come into therapy because she was depressed, was experiencing a lack of energy, was frequently late for important appointments, and was afraid she would lose her job because of it.

While I was taking Teresa's history, it came out that her mother had been an extremely abusive woman who would fly off the handle at little or no provocation. "You never knew when she was going to go off," Teresa explained. When her mother "went off," she tore into her with horrendous accusations and insults. She'd scream and yell obscenities and attack Teresa where she was most vulnerable. After such an attack, Teresa said she felt like "a Mack truck had run over me—I just felt like crawling off somewhere to die."

As a result of these constant surprise attacks, Teresa was always on the alert for any sign that her mother was getting ready to attack. This caused her body to be in a constant state of tension and stress. As a result, even when Teresa grew up and moved away from her mother, she maintained her hypervigilant frame of mind. She was always leery of other people, even her husband, constantly expecting them to attack her as her mother did. She was unable to relax her body and suffered from severe neck, shoulder, and back pain most of her life.

Because of her abusive childhood, it was impossible for Teresa to stand up for herself. As she became more and more comfortable talking with me, she shared with me that she felt her husband was overly controlling. She wanted desperately to stand up to him, but she couldn't because she was so afraid of what he would do to her.

How Fear Contributes to the Inability to Stand Up

As you can see, fear plays a significant role in women's inability to stand up for themselves. Fear can motivate women to remain helpless victims, often staying in abusive situations. Those who put up with unacceptable or abusive behavior do so out of fear of more extreme violence, fear of abandonment, fear of being alone, or sometimes, fear of their own anger.

Here are some specific ways that fear contributes to the inability to stand up for oneself:

- Those who were neglected or abandoned as children are often consumed with a fear of being alone or of being rejected or abandoned. This can cause them to put up with unacceptable or abusive behavior from others.

- Many neglected and abused children grow up to be adults who are afraid to take risks, including the risk of striking out on their own. Many people who were terrorized as children will remain dependent on their abusive parents and be unable to separate from them. Others leave their abusive parents only to attach themselves to a partner who is controlling.

- Those who are afraid they will become like an abusive parent often submerge their anger and take on a passive stance, allowing others to treat them unfairly or even to abuse them.

- Children who grow up in a climate of domination and abuse develop pathological attachments to those who abuse and neglect them, attachments they will strive to maintain even at the sacrifice of their own welfare, their own reality, or their very lives. A childhood history of placating an abusive parent or other caretaker naturally leads to placating a partner, especially an abusive one. The idea of being able to say no to the emotional demands of a partner, parent, or authority figure may be inconceivable to them. Although an adult woman does not consciously seek an abusive relationship, when abuse does occur it is often viewed by her as the inevitable price of having any relationship.

- A woman who was "trained" to believe she does not have any choices is more likely to cope than to escape.

- Children who grow up constantly afraid become immobilized by their fear. Their fear becomes so all-encompassing that it often crowds out other reactions, such as anger, that would be natural under the circumstances.

- Those raised by domineering and authoritarian parents grow up fearing their parents and were taught to equate respect with fear.

- Children who were raised in an environment of unpredictability, emotional chaos, and terror tend to grow up with the inability to trust. This may be because they did not have a secure attachment to a parent, because their parent betrayed them by crossing important personal boundaries (as in sexual abuse), or because their parents could not be relied on due to their inconsistency or neglect. In adult relationships, this lack of trust is expressed by extreme insecurity, possessiveness, and jealousy, which can translate into dependence and being unable to stand up for oneself.

Remedies

Remedy #1: Determine Why It Is So Difficult for You to Stand Up

It is important to determine whether your problem concerning standing up for yourself was caused primarily by the messages you received from society when growing up, messages (spoken and unspoken) from your parents, negative experiences when you tried to stand up for yourself in the past, or abusive experiences as a child or an adult. The following exercise will help you with this discovery.

Exercise: What Is the Source of Your Fear of Standing Up?

The following questions are meant to help you to spend some time evaluating your past and making connections between the messages and the experiences you had as a child and your behavior today.

- What messages do you remember receiving from your parents, other authority figures, and society in general about girls being assertive?

- If you were overly controlled, dominated, or abused as a child, how has the fear you felt affected you as an adult? For example, do you tend to placate those you are afraid of?

- In your determination to never become like your domineering or abusive parents, have you gone to the other extreme and submerged all assertiveness and aggression to the point that you allow others to dominate you?

- What has been your experience when you have stood up for yourself in the past?

Remedy #2: Recognize the Price You Pay for Not Standing Up

Women pay a heavy price for not standing up for themselves. They are often seen as weak by other people because they have lost their voice. In my book *Loving Him without Losing You: How to Stop Disappearing and Start Being Yourself*, I wrote about how many women complain about not being listened to, heard, or "seen" by their partner. These women often feel that their partner ignores their feelings and needs and that they are taken for granted. When they do muster enough strength to voice an opinion or to disagree with their partners, they usually have the experience of being ignored or discounted.

This is what Denise, a "disappearing" woman, told me: "I learned early in my marriage that it just wasn't worth it for me to get angry with my husband or even to disagree with him. He'd end up getting even more angry with me than I was with him. He'd rant and rave for hours, and I'd end up feeling really small. So now I just go along with whatever he says or does." Unfortunately, Denise was becoming more invisible every day. While it may have seemed hopeless to communicate her feelings to her husband, by giving up trying, she had sacrificed a part of herself in the process. And by keeping quiet, she was sending the message that it was okay for her husband to treat her inappropriately.

Some women don't give up stating their grievances altogether; they simply choose to do so in a passive way. The most common way women make their complaints known is to whine. But whining makes others perceive them as a victim, a martyr, or a loser, and causes others to lose respect for them.

By not standing up for themselves when it is appropriate, many women damage their self-esteem. They become angry with and ashamed of themselves for putting up with inappropriate behavior. The more they put up with, the worse they feel. Soon, they begin to believe they don't have the right to complain. They convince themselves they are making a big thing out of nothing, or they become so dependent that they are terrified of making their partner angry and risking being abandoned.

Women who don't stand up for themselves often develop physical and emotional illnesses. Many become depressed because they feel so hopeless and helpless about being able to change their lives and because they turn their anger inward. Many are prone to certain types of headaches, muscle tension, nervous conditions, and insomnia.

And there is another, very important price women pay for not standing up for themselves: if they continue to pretend there is no problem or to run away from an adverse situation or the abusive person, there is no way they can fix what's wrong. Not only do they neglect to find solutions to their problems but their inability to stand up for themselves often prevents them from getting what they want. Whether it is telling a partner that they are tired of sitting home every weekend or telling their boss that they need a raise, taking the risk to stand up for themselves can actually help them to have their needs met.

Exercise: The Price You've Paid

1. Make a list of all the ways you pay a price for not standing up for yourself.

2. Review this list periodically to remind yourself of how important it is to begin standing up for yourself.

Remedy #3: Begin to Overcome Your Learned Helplessness

It is especially difficult for those who were abused in childhood to act on their own behalf. Those who were victimized as a child often suffer from learned helplessness—the belief that they cannot control the outcome of any situation through their own actions. Those with this mind-set believe that nothing can be gained by standing up for one's rights or protecting oneself from harm. Therefore, even though you may feel angry about the way someone is treating you, if you have this mind-set you might think to yourself, "What good will it do to tell this person how I feel? It won't change anything."

It is very important for you to understand that the main purpose of your standing up for yourself and confronting inappropriate behavior is *not* to change the other person. The purpose is for you to stand up so that *you* will begin to feel better about yourself. Standing up to someone who is treating you poorly will help your self-esteem. It will help you to feel less powerless and less hopeless. It will help you to gain self-respect.

Fortunately, there will be times when your standing up will have a positive effect on the other person. Sometimes the other person will suddenly realize that his or her behavior was inappropriate and will therefore change it. And we know that some abusers will respect and cease to attempt to dominate women who stand up for themselves. But again, changing the other person is not the primary reason to confront him or her. Standing up is for you. It is for your self-respect and self-esteem.

Remedy #4: Learn How to Cope with Your Fear

As we discussed earlier in this chapter, there is a strong likelihood that the reason you have difficulty standing up for yourself is that you are afraid. The message of fear is that something requires your attention. It means that you need to be prepared for something. Most often, fear signals danger. Unfortunately, those who were abused as children often live their life in a state of fear, even when there is no imminent danger. If you are aware that you are feeling afraid or anxious, ask yourself if there is something currently going on in your life that you need to be afraid of or concerned about. If you cannot find anything in the present, assume it is your anxiety and fear from the past.

There are positive ways of dealing with this kind of fear based on the past:

- *Feel the fear but don't become overwhelmed by it.* You may have heard the phrase, "What you resist, persists." This can sometimes be true of fear. By simply acknowledging your fear, allowing yourself to feel it, and then breathing into it, you may be amazed at how your fear diminishes. The same is true of anxiety. Simply trying to accept it, letting yourself feel it, may be the best way to handle it. Battling with it is likely to create a greater internal struggle.

- *Ask yourself if it is appropriate to be feeling fear.* Your fear or anxiety today may be the same as you experienced in childhood abuse situations, albeit in a different form. By connecting your current fear to past experiences, you will put distance and perspective on the situation. Doing so will enable you to reduce the fear and help you work through it.

Remedy #5: Begin to Set and Enforce Better Boundaries and Limits

As clichéd as it may sound, Nice Girls need to learn to set better boundaries for themselves. They need to learn to say no more often. They need to be willing to say what they want and need, even when it inconveniences someone else.

Many of you are probably familiar with the concept of boundaries; for those of you who are not, here is a brief overview of exactly what boundaries are and how to set them. A boundary is a limit, a demarcation. Personal boundaries define the territory of your personal space. There are physical and emotional boundaries that separate us from other people. Your skin is an example of a physical boundary, since your skin creates a physical barrier that separates you from all other living and nonliving organisms. We also have an invisible boundary around our bodies that is often referred to as our "comfort zone." Our comfort zone varies, depending on the situation. For example, you are no doubt much more comfortable allowing a friend to stand close to you than you would be with a stranger.

An emotional boundary usually takes the form of a limit. We all have limits as to what feels appropriate and safe when it comes to how others treat us emotionally. What may feel fine to you may feel uncomfortable to your partner. But unless you tell your partner you are uncomfortable, he or she will never know and will continue treating you in a manner that is uncomfortable to you. This doesn't help either one of you. If you allow someone to emotionally abuse you, for example, you are not honoring and protecting your boundaries and you are participating in the erosion of your relationship.

A boundary violation occurs when someone crosses the physical or emotional limits set by another person. All relationships, even our most intimate ones, have limits as to what is appropriate. When someone crosses the line between what is appropriate and inappropriate, whether they do it knowingly or unknowingly, that person has violated our boundary.

Most of us begin a relationship thinking we have certain limits as to what we will or will not tolerate from a partner. But as the relationship progresses, we move our boundaries back, tolerating more and more intrusion or going along with things we are really opposed to. Although this can occur even in healthy relationships, in abusive ones a partner begins tolerating unacceptable or even abusive behavior and then convinces herself that these boundaries are normal and acceptable. She believes her partner when he tells her she deserves such treatment.

EXERCISE: ESTABLISHING YOUR BOUNDARIES

1. Only you can decide what you will and will not accept in your relationships. In order to set your boundaries, you need to know what they are. Spend some time thinking about the kinds of behaviors that bother you the most, that push your buttons, or that are morally unacceptable to you. Make a list of these behaviors. Your list might include such things as reading your mail, going through your private papers, making fun of you in front of others.

2. Make another list about what your personal limits are, regarding your partner's (or a child's) behavior. For example, you may think it is okay for your partner to have two drinks but no more, since you have noticed that his or her personality changes after two drinks. You came from an alcoholic family and have no intention of being involved with a heavy drinker.

Remedy #6: Learn to Communicate Your Limits and Boundaries

Now that you are clearer about what your boundaries and limits are, you will need to communicate to others what they are. You can do this in one of two ways. You can choose an appropriate time to sit down with your partner, a friend, or co-worker and explain that you have been working on establishing better boundaries. Explain why you have the limits and boundaries you have and ask that the other person honor them. You may also take this opportunity to ask your partner to share his or her boundaries and limits with you.

On the other hand, this method may seem too formal and too scary for you. You may choose instead to stand up for your limits and boundaries on a case-by-case basis. Boundary violations can be healed in the moment if you gently tell the other person about it at the time and he or she apologizes for it and assures you that it will not happen again. Unfortunately, this doesn't always happen. The other person may get defensive or deny that he or she violated your boundary. Don't let this discourage you from bringing up offenses, however. While the individual may deny the violation at the time, after thinking it over he or she may realize what he or she has done and try harder to honor your boundaries in the future. Plus, you need the practice at standing up for yourself and asserting your limits.

Remedy #7: Learn How to Say No

Learning how to say no is a type of boundary setting, but it is so important that I have created a separate remedy for it. I understand that it can be frightening to say no to someone and risk his or her anger, disapproval, or even rejection. But if you cannot say no when you need to, you risk exploitation, a loss of your self-respect, the respect of others, and even perhaps your safety.

EXERCISE: PRACTICE SAYING NO

Practice saying the word *no*. Say it out loud when you are by yourself. Say it silently to yourself whenever you would like to say it to someone out loud but are afraid to do so. If you continue practicing and telling yourself you have the right to say no, eventually you'll gain the confidence to speak your mind out loud.

As women, we certainly have come a long way. But unfortunately, many of us have not learned powerful ways to say no. Many have been hampered by the messages that we should be meek, timid, polite, and subservient. We find ourselves without the tools to resist or disagree.

Because many women are not taught how to say no, I will teach you how do so by providing actual dialogue suggestions for specific situations. These suggestions will equip you to resist, disagree, or argue without becoming aggressive.

Situation: Someone tries to pressure you into doing something.

Suggested response: "I'm not comfortable with that" or "No, I just don't want to do it."

If the person continues to pressure you: "I'd like you to respect my feelings" or "I'm not going to change my mind. I feel strongly about this."

Situation: Someone has made plans that involve you without checking with you first.

Suggested response: "That doesn't work for me. We'll have to make other arrangements."

If the person continues to pressure you: "I need you to hear me. I don't want to do that."

Remedy #8: Learn How to Be More Assertive

You've heard the word *assertive* many times, and no doubt you've heard people tell you that you should be more assertive. But this is easier said than done. Let's start by defining what assertiveness actually is. Assertiveness is an alternative to personal powerlessness and manipulation. It is a tool for making your relationships equal, for avoiding the one-down feeling that often comes when you fail to express what you really want. Being assertive also may increase your self-esteem, reduce anxiety, gain you a greater respect for yourself and others, and improve your ability to communicate more effectively with others.

There are many other benefits to assertiveness. Primarily, assertiveness aids you by:

- *Helping you to act in your own best interest.* Assertiveness encourages you to make your own decisions rather than to allow others to dictate how you should run your life. It encourages you to take initiative and to trust your own judgment.

- *Helping you to stand up for yourself.* This includes assertive behaviors such as saying no; setting limits on time and energy; responding to criticism, put-downs, or anger; and stating and defending your opinions.

- *Helping you to express your feelings honestly and comfortably.* This includes being able to disagree, to show anger, to admit to fear or anxiety, or to be spontaneous without painful anxiety.

- *Helping you to stand up for your rights.* This includes the ability to respond to violations of your rights or those of others and the ability to work for change.

- *Helping you to respect the rights of others.* Ultimately, assertiveness is the ability to accomplish all of the above without hurting others, being unfairly critical of others, or having to revert to manipulation or controlling behavior.

To learn how to stand up for yourself and express your feelings directly and honestly, it may be necessary to overcome certain beliefs about assertiveness, such as:

- *Believing you don't have a right to be assertive.* Even though you may have learned otherwise, we all have a right to be assertive about getting our needs met. Assertiveness does not mean you have the right to take advantage of other people in order to take care of yourself or that you have the right to insist on having things your own way. What it does mean is that you have the right to stand up for yourself and look after your own interests, the same as everyone else.

- *Believing that being assertive will turn people off.* Many people are reluctant to be more assertive because they are afraid people will think of them as overbearing, pushy, or obnoxious. If you live your life to please everyone else, you will continue to feel frustrated and powerless. This is because what others want may not be what is good for you. You are not being mean when you say no to unreasonable demands or when you express your ideas, feelings, and opinions, even if they differ from those of others. Asserting yourself will not upset people as much as you think it will, and even if it does, they will get over it. When you decide to make changes in the way you deal with people you will be surprised at how quickly they will get used to your new approach. Some people will actually prefer the new you.

- *Overcoming familial and cultural negativity about being assertive.* This can be a difficult process. We discussed the problems women have in overcoming the cultural expectation that they remain passive. The messages you received from your family or your childhood experiences may have also caused you to believe that assertiveness is unacceptable or even dangerous. Practice telling yourself the following to counter these messages:

1. I have the right to be treated with respect by others.
2. I have the right to express my feelings (including anger) and opinions.
3. I have the right to say no without feeling guilty.
4. I have the right to ask for what I want.
5. I have the right to make my own mistakes.
6. I have the right to pursue happiness.

So how do you become more assertive? You start by saying no. You start by speaking up when someone does something or says something that is offensive to you. Although there are suggested formats for being assertive, it can be as simple as standing up for yourself.

What you say and the way you say it makes all the difference between being heard and being ignored or dismissed. It is not necessary to put the other person down (aggressive) to express your feelings (assertive). It is important to express yourself and take responsibility for your feelings, not to blame the other person for how you feel. An assertive statement to communicate anger needs to contain two thoughts:

• The fact that you are angry or concerned and the reason for it.
• What you want the other person to do about it.

A simple form for such a statement is, "I feel concerned (or angry) because _____. I would like you to _____."

Every situation is different, of course, and so the words may differ. Be sure to follow these simple rules:

1. Practice being assertive by making your needs and grievances known. Instead of withholding your anger or whining, state your grievances when they first come up in as honest a way as you can. In a very direct, assertive way, make your needs known.

2. Avoid using "you," "always," and "never" statements, such as: "You never take me out anymore" or "You always make fun of me" (these words can shame the other person and make them feel hopeless, misunderstood, or defensive). Instead use "I" statements, such as "I would appreciate it if we could go out at least once a month" or "I don't like it when you make fun of me."

3. Avoid name-calling, insults, or sarcasm.

4. If you confront someone about inappropriate behavior, don't back down. If you end up giving in, the next time the person behaves in the same inappropriate way, your words of confrontation will mean nothing. The other person will just assume you are "spouting off" and that he or she doesn't need to take you seriously. State your position and stick to it. Don't back down and don't apologize for bringing up the issue.

5. There is also no need to argue about what you have said. If the other person defends him- or herself, listen carefully and then say something like "I understand you don't agree with me and you have a right to your point of view. But I would appreciate it if you'd think about what I've said."

6. Be consistent and state consequences. For example, don't complain endlessly about someone's excessive drinking and then get drunk with him or her one night. And don't threaten to end a relationship unless you are willing to stand by your words. Otherwise you'll weaken your words and your position.

The following information will guide you step-by-step through the process of initiating a positive yet assertive exchange with someone you are having difficulties with or who has hurt your feelings or angered you.

1. *Start on a positive note.* When you have a complaint about a person's behavior, it is generally a good idea to start by giving the person some acknowledgment for the positive things that he or she has done or the positive aspects of the relationship. For example, "I want you to know that I really appreciate the fact that you are being less critical of me than you used to be."

2. *Then give an "I" statement that expresses your feelings and describes the problem very specifically.* Depending on the context and the

relationship, you may need to be more or less tactful. A positive example: "I don't like it when you make fun of me in front of our friends like you did last night."

3. *Avoid blaming statements.* In addition to avoiding blaming "you" statements, such as "You knew that would embarrass me," also avoid provocative, judgmental ones such as "What's wrong with you?" or "Don't you realize it made you look stupid?"

4. *Explain why you are upset.* Include any effects the person's behavior has had on you. A positive example: "It really embarrasses me when you make fun of me like that." Resist the urge to blame or whine. Just state the reasons you are upset.

5. *State your expectations clearly and specifically.* Express firmly, but in a nonblaming way, what your needs, desires, or expectations are concerning the problem. A positive example: "I would appreciate it if you would not do that again. If you do it again, I will call you on it in front of everyone."

6. *Acknowledge the other person and ask for input.* At this point you can ask the other person where he or she is coming from and for any suggestions he or she might have for solving the problem. Why not begin your encounter with this more empathetic approach, you might ask. The reason is that Nice Girls generally have too much empathy for others and not enough empathy for themselves. They also get easily side-tracked by others' perspectives and excuses. Once you have let off some steam and made your needs and expectations clear, you can better afford to listen to the other person's point of view and give him or her a chance to be a problem-solving collaborator. A positive example: "Thank you for listening to me. Now I'd really like to hear what you have to say about the situation and what suggestions you might have to solve the problem."

There are other aspects of behavior that can contribute to the success of an assertive exchange. For an interaction to be effective, follow these guidelines:

1. *Have good eye contact.* Looking directly at the person as you speak helps to communicate your sincerity and improves the directness of your message. On the other hand, if you

look down or away most of the time, you project a lack of confidence.

2. *Notice your flow of speech.* Clear and slow comments are more easily understood and more powerful than rapid speech that is erratic and filled with long pauses.

3. *Notice your body posture.* An active and erect posture while facing the other person directly will lend additional impact to your message. In some situations in which you are called upon to stand up for yourself, it may be helpful to do just that— stand up. This will undoubtedly give you additional courage and will encourage the other person to take you more seriously and pay closer attention to what you are saying.

4. *Notice your distance and physical contact.* Distance from another person has a considerable effect upon communication. Standing or sitting very closely to another person, or touching another person, suggests intimacy in a relationship (unless you happen to be in a crowd or in a very cramped space). This can put the other person at ease, assuring him or her that although your words may be confrontational, you are still on his or her side or feeling close to the person.

5. *Pay attention to your facial expressions.* To communicate effectively and assertively, your facial expression needs to be congruent with your message and your intention. An angry message is clearest when delivered with a straight, unsmiling facial expression as opposed to a weak, smiling one. (Women often deliver their messages in this weak manner because they want to soft-pedal what they are saying). Conversely, a friendly communication should not be delivered with a dark frown, which can be intimidating. Let your face say the same things your words are saying.

6. *Pay attention to your gestures.* Accentuating your message with appropriate gestures can add emphasis, openness, and warmth. On the other hand, intense, abrupt, or threatening gestures such as finger-pointing, table-pounding, or fist-making can be intimidating or frightening.

7. *Notice your voice, tone, volume, and inflection.* The way we use our voices is a vital aspect of our communications. The same

words spoken through clenched teeth in anger offer an entirely different message than when they are whispered in fear. If you can control and use your voice effectively, you can acquire a powerful tool for self-expression. Practice speaking into a tape recorder, trying out different styles until you achieve a style you like.

8. *Notice your timing.* Hesitation often diminishes the effectiveness of your assertive statements. The more you practice being assertive, the more courage you will have to confront people at the time of the offense instead of waiting and obsessing about what you could have said. On the other hand, it is never too late to be assertive. Even though the ideal moment may have passed, you will usually find it worthwhile to go to the person later and express your feelings.

Practice being assertive in low-risk situations to build up your courage. For example, would you be more comfortable being assertive toward someone you know or toward a stranger? Would it be easier to be assertive over the telephone or in writing instead of in a face-to-face encounter?

This is what Teresa (whom you met earlier in the chapter) did as she prepared herself for becoming more assertive with her controlling husband. She began by being assertive with waitresses and store clerks. "I was so traumatized by my mother's anger that I couldn't do things like send food back that was inedible, question a bill that seemed too high, or say no to a store clerk who was pressuring me to buy something. So that's where I started. It was really difficult at first, but I kept reminding myself that the person wasn't my mother and asking myself, 'What do you have to lose?'

"It was usually easier than I had expected, and each time I did it I felt stronger and stronger—so much so that I started being more assertive with my friends. I have one friend in particular who always has to have her way. So instead of just going along with whatever she wanted to do as I had in the past, I started speaking up and saying when I didn't want to do something. At first she got really mad at me and said, 'You know, I liked you a lot better before you started going to therapy. Now you always have to have your way.' I knew, of course, that she just didn't like not getting her way, so I just said, 'Yeah, I'm sure it was a lot nicer for you when I just went along with you all the time. But this is the new me, so get used to it.' To my surprise, she actually started treating me with more respect.

"This gave me the courage and resolve to try being assertive with my husband. I followed the format you'd given me and it really worked! Instead of talking to him in my usual weak, scared way, I actually made my voice stronger and looked him straight in the eye. I told him that I didn't like the fact that he completely controlled our finances and that I'd like for both of us to decide how we are going to spend our money. I also told him I wanted to be able to have a checkbook of my own.

"He got really angry and said that I didn't know how to manage money and that I'd get the bookkeeping all messed up because I wouldn't record all the checks I write. I did get scared when he raised his voice, but I reminded myself that he wasn't my mother, and I didn't back down. I told him we could get the kind of checkbook that has a built-in carbon copy so that he wouldn't have to worry about that. This seemed to surprise him and shut him up. He ended up saying, 'Well I guess we can give it a try.'

"I think he could sense that I just wasn't as afraid of him as I always had been before. To tell you the truth, I think that made the difference as much as my being more assertive."

Remedy #9: Recognize Signs of Abuse in Its Early Stages

While it is important for all Nice Girls to learn to be assertive, it is especially vital that you learn to stand up for yourself if someone close to you is being emotionally abusive. Emotional abuse is an insidious form of abuse that sneaks up on people and often precedes physical abuse. Because Nice Girls have difficulty standing up for themselves, many find themselves in abusive relationships without even realizing it. This doesn't have to be your situation. There are certain behaviors that are both indicators of emotional abuse and warning signs that more serious forms of emotional or even physical abuse could occur in the future if something is not done to change the dynamics in the relationship.

1. Does your partner tend to embarrass or make fun of you in front of your friends, family, or in-laws?

2. Does he or she tend to put down your accomplishments and goals?

3. Does he or she frequently question your decisions or ability to make decisions?

4. Does your partner always take the opposite view of whatever you say?

5. When you try to discuss an issue with your partner, does he or she get angry or cut you down by saying he or she doesn't know what you're talking about?

6. Does your partner use intimidation or threats to get you to do as he or she wishes?

7. Has your partner ever said or implied that you are nothing without him or her or that you were nothing until he or she came along?

8. Does your partner treat you roughly when he or she is upset, such as pushing or shoving you?

9. Does your partner call you several times a night or show up to make sure you are where you said you would be?

10. Does your partner use alcohol or drugs to excess?

11. Does he or she get into arguments with you while drinking?

12. Does your partner tend to blame you for everything that goes wrong in his or her life?

13. Does your partner pressure you sexually—either for things you are not ready for or to have sex more often than you would like?

14. Does your partner insinuate that there is no way out of the relationship—meaning that he or she will not let you go?

15. Does your partner prevent you from doing things you want to do—like spending time with your friends or family members?

16. Has your partner tried to keep you from leaving during a fight?

17. Has your partner ever abandoned you somewhere during a fight, to "teach you a lesson"?

18. Have you ever been afraid of how your partner was acting or what he or she was capable of doing?

19. Do you feel like, no matter what you do or how hard you try, your partner is never happy with you?

20. Do you always feel like you are walking on eggshells, trying to avoid a conflict or making your partner angry?

If you answered yes to many of these questions, your relationship is either emotionally abusive or is heading in that direction. In a healthy relationship, these kinds of interactions do not occur on a regular basis. Instead, both partners feel supported and respected by each other as opposed to feeling threatened, embarrassed, or criticized. Both partners allow each other the space and the freedom necessary to maintain their separate sense of self. And instead of feeling threatened by the other's successes, they feel genuinely happy for their partner.

If you are currently being emotionally abused, you absolutely must start standing up for yourself. The more you allow someone to treat you in inappropriate and abusive ways, the less this person will respect you and the less you will respect yourself.

If you are being emotionally abused, you need to ask yourself what you are willing to do to stop the abuse. Are you willing (and able) to stand up to your partner and confront him or her about the abusive behavior? Are you willing (and able) to establish clearer boundaries with your partner? If you are not able to do either of these things, are you willing to end a relationship that is clearly a destructive one to you and your children?

If you are confused as to what emotional abuse looks like in adult relationships, refer to my books *The Emotionally Abusive Relationship* and *The Emotionally Abused Woman*. These books will also offer you help in how to confront abusive behavior and how to leave an abusive relationship.

10

Start Expressing Your Anger

Anger is an acid that can do more harm to the
vessel in which it is stored than to anything
on which it is poured.

—MARK TWAIN

False belief: Anger is a destructive emotion and shouldn't
be expressed, especially directly to those to whom you are
angry.

Empowering belief: Anger is a healthy emotion, or I have a
right to my anger.

*This chapter is beneficial for
all types of Nice Girls*

Nice Girls don't believe in anger. Some think that getting angry
is inappropriate and a sign that a person is out of control.
Others are afraid of anger—that of others as well as their own. They
are afraid that if they get angry, they will be rejected or abandoned
by others. They are afraid that they will lose control and hurt someone. But allowing yourself to get angry and to express your anger in
constructive ways is one of the most healthy and empowering things
a Nice Girl can do.

Societal Reasons Girls and Women Have Difficulty Expressing Anger Directly

While we all have our individual reasons for our fear or avoidance of anger, there are some powerful societal reasons that girls and women find it difficult, if not impossible, to express their anger in direct ways.

There is considerable disagreement as to whether this difficulty is caused by gender differences or status and power discrepancies. It is likely a combination of the two. For example, some contend that our society permits women the expression of anger in defense of those more vulnerable than themselves (such as their children) but discourages them from expressing anger on their own behalf (probably rooted in the belief that women's power unleashed is considered devastating). It is also clear that women have been trained to contain their anger when they are being violated, in fear of retaliation by those more powerful.

Researchers such as Belenky and Gilligan have found that connection with others is primary for women. With this in mind, it becomes clear why a woman will go to any lengths, including altering herself, to establish and maintain intimate ties.

According to Belenky and Gilligan: "Not a lot has changed when it comes to how we raise our daughters regarding anger. While aggression is the symbol of masculinity and boys still get their peers' respect for athletic prowess, resisting authority, and acting tough, dominating, and confident, girls are expected to mature into caregivers—a role deeply at odds with aggression. Girls gain their peers' respect by being sweet, caring, and tender—in other words, caretakers in training. 'Good girls' are not supposed to experience anger because aggression endangers relationships, thus impeding a girl's ability to be caring and 'nice.'"

Research shows that parents and teachers discourage the emergence of physical and direct aggression in girls early on, whereas the rough-housing and skirmishing of boys is either encouraged or shrugged off. For example, a 1999 University of Michigan study found that girls were told to be quiet, speak softly, or use a "nice" voice about three times more often than were boys, even though the boys were louder. By the time they are school age, children have created social groups that value niceness in girls and toughness in boys.

Our culture also derides aggression in girls as being unfeminine. Assertive girls are called "bitch," "lesbian," "frigid," and "manly."

To many, the word *nice* really means "not aggressive, not angry." For many years, it was considered fact that girls were simply not inherently aggressive. This was because the first experiments on aggression were performed with almost no female subjects. Since males tend to exhibit aggression directly, researchers concluded that aggression was expressed only in this way. Other forms of aggression (such as gossiping or ignoring someone), when they were observed, were labeled deviant or ignored.

The rules are different for boys, and the girls know it. For girls, overt displays of aggression are punished by social rejection. But try as they may, most girls cannot erase the natural impulse toward anger that every human being has. In *Odd Girl Out*, Rachel Simmons noted a study of girls in 1992 conducted by Norwegian researchers, which revealed that girls were not at all averse to aggression; they just expressed anger in unconventional ways. The group predicted that "when aggression cannot, for one reason or another, be directed (physically or verbally) at its target, the perpetrator has to find other channels." The findings bore out their theory: cultural rules against overt aggression led girls to engage in other, nonphysical forms of aggression. The researchers challenged the image of sweetness among female youths, calling their social lives "ruthless," "aggressive," and "cruel."

Girls and women are not only discouraged from expressing anger because it is "unladylike" but because they often sense that their anger would do terrible damage if they let it out. To some degree they are right. When people feel they have no rights, when they consistently give more than they receive, they become very angry. The longer that anger is suppressed, the more powerful and potent it can become. When people are finally pushed to their limits, they often explode in verbal or physical violence. We see this happen with battered women who end up killing their abusers.

It is often the case that the weaker a person feels, the more dangerous she feels. While weakness may be what a woman feels who is being emotionally or physically abused, in reality, one of the reasons she may not stand up for herself is that she might be afraid of losing control of her own rage.

When the Cause of Your Inability to Express Anger Lies in Childhood

Carly came to see me because she had been involved with several abusive men and she wanted to make sure that it didn't happen again. "I don't know why I continue picking these kinds of guys. I mean, I wasn't abused as a kid or anything. My parents treated me very well. I know I don't deserve to be treated like I've been by men. I want to get to the bottom of this."

As I took Carly's history, I noticed right away that she seemed to have what therapists call "flat affect." This means that she didn't seem to express much emotion. Even when she described something that was quite sad, she didn't show a hint of sadness. And as she described the abusive relationships she had experienced with men, she didn't express any anger. I finally asked her, "Carly, do you feel any anger toward these abusive men?"

Her answer was a flat "No."

"Don't you think you have a right to be angry at them?" I asked.

"Yes, I suppose I do," she answered, again with no emotion in her voice.

"Then why do you think you aren't angry?" I pressed.

"I don't know. I don't feel very many feelings at all. In fact, I feel pretty numb."

Being numb to their feelings can be a common side effect of women having been emotionally or physically abused, and I assumed that this might be part of the reason for Carly's disconnection from her emotions. I explained this to her and assured her that most people who have been traumatized do come to reconnect with their feelings, given enough time to heal from the trauma and sufficient time and experiences to regain their sense of safety. "The truth is, I've always been a bit numb to my feelings, though," Carly offered.

When I asked her to tell me more about this, she explained that while her parents had always treated her very well, there were many times when she had witnessed her mother erupting in a rage toward her father. "It scared me to see my mother get angry like that. Her anger was so unpredictable. It always came out of the blue with no notice whatsoever."

I explained to Carly that even though she had not been mistreated by her parents, witnessing one parent emotionally abusing another can be just as traumatizing as experiencing emotional abuse firsthand. I also explained that having a parent who erupts in a rage can be extremely traumatic and can cause the observer to dissociate or disconnect from his or her feelings.

"I think you might be right about that," Carly conceded. "When my mother would go on a rampage, I would go in my room and hide. I didn't cry or anything. I just sat on my bed like a robot, waiting for the yelling to stop. Then when it was all over, I just went about my life like nothing had happened."

Once it sank in that she had actually been traumatized by her mother's outbursts, Carly began to realize why she had been attracted to men who were abusive and that she had, in fact, chosen men who were like her mother in many ways. She now understood better why she was so numb to her feelings. But there was one more piece of the puzzle she had yet to discover.

During our sessions, I often pressed Carly to identify and express her feelings. For example, I would ask her, "What are you feeling right now?" or "Are you feeling angry about that?" Usually she was unable to identify her feelings, although she was getting better at it. But she seldom acknowledged that she was feeling angry. One day when I asked her if she was feeling angry, she said, "I do *feel* angry at times, you know. I just can't *express* my anger."

This was new to me and I requested that she elaborate. "I sometimes get angry at my friends or even at my parents. But I can't tell them I'm angry."

"Why is that?" I asked.

"I don't know. I think it is because I don't want to become like my mother. Yes, that's it. I'm afraid if I start telling people I'm angry, I'll become just like my mother. I'll start yelling and screaming all the time."

Carly had experienced an important breakthrough. She had been so afraid of becoming like her mother that she had gone to the opposite extreme. This is a common tactic for many. In their attempt to separate from their parents and guarantee they will be different from them, they act in opposite ways. Unfortunately, this prevents them from really breaking free—they are still responding to their parents' behavior.

Thus, we discovered that while one of the reasons Carly was numb to her feelings was that she had learned to dissociate when traumatized by her mother's rage, another reason was that she refused to express her anger. I explained to Carly that we can't just pick and choose which emotions we are going to feel. If we decide to cut ourselves off from our so-called negative emotions, such as sadness, anger, fear, and guilt, we also limit our ability to feel the so-called positive feelings of love, happiness, and joy.

But Carly continued having difficulty believing that it was okay to feel and express anger. I sensed that she needed to be educated about anger in order to be able to give herself permission to feel and express it. She needed to learn the difference between hostility and anger, and healthy and unhealthy anger. As I detailed to her, although anger clearly has some connection with hostility and aggression, they are not the same. Hostility is an *attitude* of ill will, aggression refers to *behavior* that is always meant to hurt, whereas anger is an *emotion*—plain and simple.

The Truth about Anger

As I explained to Carly, anger is neither a positive nor a negative emotion; it is the way we handle our anger—what we do with it—that makes it negative or positive. For example, when we use our anger to motivate us to make life changes or to make changes to dysfunctional systems, anger becomes a very positive emotion.

When we express our anger through aggressive or passive-aggressive ways (such as getting even or gossiping), it becomes a negative emotion. Although there are many ways to turn anger into a negative emotion, the following methods of dealing with anger cause the most problems both for the giver and the receiver and are the most common ways that women deal with anger.

Misplacing anger: When we take out anger that is meant for one person on another, we are misplacing it. We all misplace or misdirect our anger from time to time, sometimes consciously and sometimes unconsciously. Your boss bawls you out for being late again and you end up snapping at your co-workers; your husband criticizes the way you are managing money and you blow up at your teenage daughter for talking on the phone too long. We all need to curb our tendency to misdirect our anger in such ways and apologize to those we have hurt in the process. But it is when we misplace our anger on a regular basis, when we consistently avoid dealing with the people we are really angry with by discharging it on innocent people, that it becomes a real problem.

Holding in anger: It is also unhealthy when we take the anger that should be directed at someone else and turn it against ourselves. Let's say someone criticizes you or falsely accuses you of something. What do you do? Do you remain quiet, believe what they are saying about you, and begin to feel bad about yourself? Or do you get angry and tell the person you don't appreciate her criticism? If what the person is saying isn't true, do you confront her with the truth or do you begin to doubt your own perceptions and begin to believe her lies? In this case, anger held in can be a very negative thing indeed.

Denying your anger: Many women, in particular, deny they are angry, while others feel anger consciously yet choose to squelch it. They may do so because they are afraid that if they allow themselves to become angry, they will lose control and damage property or hurt someone. Or, they may be critical of people who express their anger and feel morally superior to them. From their perspective, if they were to express their anger openly, it would seem like an indication that they were weak, out of control, or less evolved.

This is what my client Holly told me: "I begin to get angry at someone, and then I switch it off—just like that. I start thinking about why they are the way they are, what their childhood was like, or what obstacles or problems they've had to face in life, and I am suddenly overwhelmed with empathy for them." While this may sound like a very evolved way of dealing with anger, in actuality, it wasn't really working for Holly. She exuded a great deal of silent hostility. You could feel it just by being in her presence. She kicked her leg almost continuously and frequently made disapproving faces and gestures. When I would note her angry gestures and ask her what she was feeling, she would usually say she wasn't feeling anything. "People always think I'm angry when I'm really not," she explained. "I guess I just have that kind of face."

Why We Need Anger

So why do we need anger at all? Why not simply work toward eliminating it from our lives entirely? The reason is that there are many positive functions of anger:

- It energizes us and motivates us to make changes in our lives.

- It serves as a catalyst for resolving interpersonal conflict.

- It promotes self-esteem—when we stand up for ourselves, we feel better about ourselves.

- It fosters a sense of personal control during times of peak stress.

- Expression of anger can actually promote health. Women with cancer who express their anger are found to live longer than those who express no anger.

- Anger and even rage can be a survival tool and a grounding technique by which women become centered and reconnected to themselves.

- As uncomfortable as anger is for many of us, it can be preferable to anxiety, as it lays the blame outside ourselves.

If we find constructive ways of releasing anger and safe places to let it out, it can becomes a positive force in our lives, creating energy, motivation, assertiveness, empowerment, and creativity.

Biologically, anger is defined as a stress response to internal or external demands, threats, and pressures. Anger warns us that there is a problem or a potential threat. At the same time, it energizes us to face the problem or meet the threat and provides us with the power to overcome it. In other words, it is both a warning system and a survival mechanism.

Our first reaction to a perceived threat is fear. When we are faced with a threat to our survival, our nervous system prepares us to meet that threat by raising our defenses. This occurs instantly and automatically, without our conscious intent. This built-in defense mechanism is found in the sympathetic branch of our autonomic nervous system, which is primarily responsible for expending physical energy and for preparing us to protect ourselves. The defense response is triggered by the release of the hormone adrenaline, which helps us out by giving us an energetic boost. This energy boost provides us with added strength and endurance to fight off our enemies or added speed with which to run from them. This pattern of biological arousal is known as the *fight-or-flight response*, an involuntary mechanism shared with all other species of animals.

Although it may not actually be part of a life-or-death struggle, we often feel threatened by the behavior or remarks of others; in other words, we experience a threat to our emotional well-being. When someone hurts or insults us by saying something inappropriate, disrespectful, or vicious, we become righteously angry.

Our anger may also signal to us that we are not addressing an important emotional issue in our lives or in a relationship. It may be a message that our wants or needs are not being met, or it may warn us that we are giving too much or compromising too much of our values or beliefs in a relationship.

I am happy to report that as Carly became aware that there is indeed a difference between anger and hostility, and that expressing anger can actually be a positive and healthy thing, she allowed herself to own and express her anger more and more, a little at a time.

This is what she shared with me just before she terminated therapy: "I could have never imagined when I first came into therapy that I would ever feel like expressing anger could be a good thing. Anger was so negative to me—the only way I'd ever seen anyone express it was the way my mother had. Now I know that there are lots of positive ways to express it and that it actually feels good to do it. I feel so much more alive now that I can express my anger. I was like the walking dead before. Thank you so much for helping me come back to life."

You, too, can "come back to life" if you tend to be numb from not expressing your feelings, including your feelings of anger. You, too, can change your mind about anger. And you, too, can learn healthy ways of expressing anger. The following remedies will help.

Remedies

Remedy #1: Discover the Origin of Your Beliefs about Anger

I believe it is safe to say that every woman has been affected to some degree by negative cultural conditioning concerning anger. Various reasons are presented in literature for the repression of anger in women. These include:

- The fear that the expression of anger will cause retaliation
- The fear that expressing anger will deny the nurturing aspect of women's socialization or drive away the love and closeness women seek
- The fear that anger, in signaling that something is wrong, calls for the necessity of change
- The need to be seen as the "good woman" or the "nice lady" as opposed to being perceived as unfeminine or the "bitch"

Put a checkmark next to each reason that you feel might be affecting your ability to express your anger directly.

We often "inherit" the way we cope with anger and our beliefs about anger from our parents' example, from their beliefs, and from the way they treated us. Some people, like Carly, fear repeating one or both of their parents' ways of expressing anger to such an extent that it causes them to take on the opposite anger style. The following exercise will help you identify any patterns you may have established based on parental messages and your parents' behavior.

EXERCISE: YOUR ANGER LEGACY

1. List the ways your mother and father dealt with their anger. Which of your parents do you feel handles anger the best?

2. List the messages you received from your family about expressing anger. For example, was it acceptable or unacceptable to confront someone when you were angry? Were you ever punished for expressing your anger? Were you ever rewarded for not expressing your anger?

3. Which of your parents do you most resemble when it comes to expressing your own anger? List the ways you are like this parent in terms of anger expression.

4. Which of your parents do you most resemble when it comes to dealing with other people's anger? List the ways you are like this parent in terms of the way he or she reacted to anger.

This exercise may have unearthed some painful truths for you. As much as we try hard to be different from our parents, especially a parent who was explosive or abusive or who put up with the abuse of others, we often become more like that parent than we care to admit. If you have found this to be true, don't be discouraged. Now that you are aware of the similarities, you can do something about it.

Remedy #2: Identify the Mistakes You Make Concerning Anger

In my experience working with female clients, I have found that women tend to make certain predictable mistakes when it comes to anger. These are:

1. Crying when you are really angry

2. Telling yourself you don't have a right to be angry

3. Telling yourself you aren't really angry even though you know you are

4. Becoming an anger magnet—that is, attracting those who will act out your anger for you

5. Pretending to forgive someone when all the while you're plotting ways to get back at him or her

6. Becoming withdrawn or distant from the person you are angry with

7. Taking the anger you feel at someone else out on yourself (by becoming self-critical or by blaming yourself)

8. Stuffing down your anger (by overeating, drinking too much, smoking cigarettes, taking drugs, shoplifting, becoming addicted to sex)

9. Taking the anger you have at one person out on someone else (becoming impatient with your children even though you are really angry with your husband)

10. Holding your anger in and then suddenly exploding in a rage and saying hurtful things to those around you

Put a checkmark beside each of the mistakes you personally make regarding anger.

As you will notice, most of the mistakes women make concerning their anger involve expressing their anger in passive rather than assertive or even aggressive ways (with the exception of number 10).

Because the expression of anger has been socially unacceptable for women, they have learned to disguise or transform their anger into hurt, sadness and worry, attempts to control, or headaches, insomnia, ulcers, back pain, and obesity. When women are under stress, anger is often turned into tears, hurt, self-doubt, silent submission, or nonproductive blaming; they often become distant or under- or overachieving.

When women do become angry, it is often accompanied by crying, an expression of the impotence and powerlessness many of them feel when victimized by injustice. Tears also accompany anger when there is a power differential between a woman and the object of her anger, when action is denied because the forces that frustrate her are too powerful. Often misinterpreted as a sign of sorrow, crying is a signal of the righteousness of women's anger along with the strength of the hurt.

Women make another mistake about anger: they confuse anger with blame. Many people, especially those with a passive anger style, believe that it is wrong to get angry. They think it is a sign of weakness or evidence of a less-than-evolved spirit. One of the reasons for this is that they confuse anger with blame. Whereas anger is a natural, healthy emotion when ventilated properly, blame is a wasted and negative experience. As noted earlier, the difference between anger and blame is that blaming keeps us caught up in the problem, while releasing our anger constructively allows us to work through the problem.

Continually blaming others for what they have done to you keeps you stuck in the past. But when you release your anger in healthy ways (such as writing anger letters that you do not send) toward those who have hurt or damaged you, you are able to step out of blame and let go of the past.

Remedy #3: Face Your Fear of Anger

It is very likely that the main reason you do not allow yourself to be angry is that you are afraid of anger. To begin to overcome this fear, it is important to understand the specific reasons for it. These can include any or all of the following:

- *The fear of retaliation.* If you were punished when you were a child every time you got angry, if you were emotionally or physically abused as a child or were a witness to abuse, or if you have been the victim of emotional or physical abuse as an adult, it makes sense that you would have this fear. As one client told me, "I remember standing up to my dad one time when I was a kid. It was the first and last time I ever did that. He slapped me across the face so hard that I went flying across the room. I learned my lesson. I never stood up to him again, or to anyone else for that matter."

- *The fear of rejection.* This is also a very real fear if you experienced rejection when you stood up for yourself. My client Janette told me about her experience with this: "My mother would stop talking to me whenever I got angry with her as a child. Sometimes she wouldn't talk to me for days until I finally apologized to her. Because of that experience, I am always afraid someone will reject me completely if I let them know I'm angry."

- *The fear of hurting another person.* My client Annie told me about her fear of hurting others: "When I first got married, I used to try to tell my husband when I was unhappy about something he'd done. But he said that if I loved him I should accept him as he was and that it upset him too much when I became angry. What he said made sense, and I didn't want him to feel so bad, so I stopped telling him when I was angry or when I didn't like something he did." This fear can be especially powerful if you have, in fact, hurt someone in the past when you were angry. This is what Carmen shared with me: "When I was growing up, I had a bad temper. I used to yell and scream and throw things when I got mad. One day I got so mad at my younger brother that I threw a plate of food at him. The plate hit him in the head and cut it open. He had to be taken to the hospital for stitches. Since that time, I've never gotten angry again."

- *The fear of becoming like those who abused you.* If you were emotionally, physically, or sexually abused as a child, your primary reason for not expressing your anger is probably your fear that you will become an abuser yourself, or at the very least that you will lose control of yourself and act in ways that you would find unacceptable. This is a genuine concern, since many who were abused do become abusive themselves. But if you fear continuing the cycle of abuse, there is even more reason for you to begin to communicate openly about your angry feelings. If you continue to hold in your anger, it is likely that you may one day explode in a rage. It is also likely that you may already be taking your anger out on your loved ones (for example, by belittling or berating, punishing in silence, or having unreasonable expectations). Your old, repressed anger toward those who mistreated you needs to be released in constructive ways, and your current anger needs to be expressed openly. Then, and only then, can you ensure that you will not become like those who abused you.

- *The fear of losing control.* It may seem to you that expressing or communicating your anger is a form of losing control. You may be afraid that once you begin to express your anger, you will go crazy and hurt others or yourself. Ironically, it is often the person who represses his or her anger who is most likely to become destructive or to have rage erupt in inappropriate ways, at inappropriate times. You will not go crazy if you allow yourself to feel and express your anger. If you learn to consistently allow yourself to express your anger instead of holding it in, you will find that you will actually feel *more in control* of your emotions and yourself, instead of less.

- *The fear of becoming irrational or making a fool of yourself.* Far from making you irrational, becoming angry can often cause you to think and see things more clearly. It can also empower you to make needed changes in your life. This is especially true if you don't allow your anger to build up to the point where you lose it and begin to yell, act irrationally, or lash out at someone.

Exercise: Getting Past Your Resistance

1. Make a list of the reasons you are afraid of your anger.

2. Write and complete this sentence: "I don't want to express my anger because _____." Don't think about your answers beforehand, just write. Continue completing this sentence for as long as you have responses.

Remedy #4: Look for Other Reasons You Don't Allow Yourself to Be Angry

Sometimes people deny their anger because if they were to acknowledge it, they would also feel the separation that comes with anger. Anger separates people—it creates a distance between people. Those who deny their anger are often enmeshed with the people in their lives—their parents, their spouse, their children. Enmeshment is an unhealthy connection with someone, indicating overinvolvement, a loss of self, or an inability to emotionally separate from the person. Young children often deny their anger toward their parents because they don't want to feel separate from them. This is normal and healthy. But as we mature, we need to feel separate from our parents to develop an individualized sense of self. This is why it is typical and healthy for adolescents to frequently feel angry with their parents. It is part of what is referred to as the individuation process.

Unfortunately, some adolescents don't go through this normal stage of development. They remain enmeshed with their parents, refusing to acknowledge or express their anger toward them for fear of feeling separate from them. Ironically, it is often those children who have been neglected or abused by their parents who have the most difficulty getting angry and separating. This is because they tenaciously hold onto the hope of getting what they didn't get while they were growing up. As long as they hold onto this hope they can't afford to get angry.

This same phenomenon occurs when someone is too enmeshed with a partner. If a battered wife were to admit that she was angry with her abusive husband, she might have to face the fact that she needs to leave him. If she is totally dependent on him either emotionally or financially or both, she can't afford to risk feeling her anger. If an overly dependent woman whose partner continually flirts with other women were to admit her anger, she might have to face the possibility that her partner does not love her. If she were to confront him with her anger, she would also risk finding out how he really feels about her.

In order to risk feeling our anger, we need to be willing to feel our separateness from the person we are angry with. If we don't want to feel that separation, we can't afford to acknowledge or feel our anger. This is why feeling and expressing anger is often the first step to releasing yourself from an unhealthy situation or relationship. You need to begin to untangle yourself from the feeling of enmeshment and learn that you have a separate identify. You need to learn that you can survive as a separate person.

Remedy #5: Express Buried Emotions from the Past

Unexpressed and buried emotions from the past can interfere with your life today. It may be necessary for you to find a way to uncover and express your repressed anger to free yourself from the past, find your voice, and live more assertively in the present. There are many ways of voicing your anger and pain from the past. Here are some suggestions:

- Write about your anger concerning significant negative events from your childhood. Getting your feelings down in black and white can act as a catharsis, helping you to get the feelings out instead of continuing to allow them to fester and grow inside you.

- Write a letter to each of the people who hurt you in the past. Don't censor yourself. Say everything that comes to mind and don't hold anything back—even your most hateful feelings. The purpose of the letter is to help you come out of denial, face the truth about what happened to you and how you feel about it, and eventually allow you to gain some closure. You need not mail the letter; in fact, it is best if you do not. If you wish, you can keep these letters for future reference, or tear them up, or burn them as a symbolic act of closure.

- Pretend that those who hurt you in the past are standing in front of you. Tell each person exactly what he or she did to hurt you, how those actions or inaction harmed you, and how you feel about him or her now.

Your repressed anger, once found, can be a treasure that provides you with a wonderful avenue for healing. Your anger can provide you the strength, the motivation, and the resolve to heal unfinished childhood issues and to start your life anew. It can provide you with the courage to confront the people and situations in your life that are unhealthy or abusive.

Remedy #6: Give Yourself Permission to Release Your Anger Physically

The previous suggestions for releasing old anger can be highly effective. But for some people, anger needs to be released physically. If you sense this is true for you, ask your body what it needs to do to release your anger. We often have an intuitive sense that we need to throw or kick or hit something. If that is the case, find a way to do this safely. Here are some suggestions:

- Use your fists to hit your bed, or get an old tennis racket and hit it against your bed or some large pillows.
- Buy some cheap dishes or some skeet (lightweight objects used for target practice) and throw them against your garage walls.
- Place a large pillow on the floor up against your couch or bed. Lie on your back and place your feet up against the pillow and push as hard as you can. (This is extremely effective for someone who was sexually abused as a child or raped as an adult.)

Backed-up anger—anger that has often been held down since childhood and then has been constantly added on to—is unhealthy. When we are very young children, we didn't hang on to our feelings and let them grow. Instead, we let them out immediately. We screamed, we cried, we kicked our legs, we had a temper tantrum. Give yourself permission to have a temper tantrum. Lie on the bed and flail your arms and legs. Make fists of your hands and punch them down hard on the bed. Move your head from side to side and let the sounds that are bubbling up come out of your mouth.

Remedy #7: Recognize the Damage You Cause Yourself and Others by Not Expressing Your Anger

If you have a tendency to repress or suppress your anger, you have lost touch with an important part of yourself. Getting angry is a way to gain back that part of yourself by asserting your rights, expressing your displeasure with a situation, and letting others know how you wish to be treated. It can motivate you to make needed changes in a relationship or other areas of your life. Finally, it can let others know that you expect to be respected and treated fairly.

Don't fool yourself into thinking that just because you don't express your anger, it will miraculously go away. Each emotion has a purpose, and that emotion will remain with you, buried inside your body, locked up in your psyche, until that purpose is recognized and understood. Anger arises within us to tell us that what is occurring is undesirable or unhealthy. Suppressing your emotions—that is, consciously trying to bury them—does not eliminate them. In addition to causing you to become numb to your feelings, including your positive feelings, your suppressed emotions will often cause physical symptoms such as muscle tension, back problems, stomach distress, constipation, diarrhea, headaches, obesity, or maybe even hypertension.

Your suppressed anger may also cause you to overreact to people and situations or to act inappropriately. Unexpressed anger can cause you to become irritable, irrational, and prone to emotional outbursts and episodes of depression. If you carry around a lot of suppressed or repressed anger (anger you have unconsciously buried), you may lash out at people, blaming or punishing them for something someone else did long ago. Because you were unwilling or unable to express how you felt in the past, you may overreact in the present, damaging your relationships.

The passive anger style is not compatible with a healthy relationship. Denying you are angry or withdrawing from your partner does not give the two of you the chance to work out your problems. Instead, you are likely to build up tension and then finally blow up. After your tirade, your partner is likely to feel wounded and angry and wonder why in the world you didn't say something before.

It is also important to realize that as long as you are angry, you will exude a certain kind of angry energy. Sometimes this energy is palpable and is consciously experienced by others. Other times, it is felt only subliminally by others, but it is felt nevertheless. People are affected by your anger whether it is overt or not and whether they are aware of it or not. They will respond by getting angry along with you, by acting out your anger for you, or by being on guard around you.

Not responding to someone's provocation, turning the other cheek, or "letting things go" won't stop the other person from continuing his or her unacceptable behavior. It won't make the individual back off and leave you alone. In fact, reacting passively to inappropriate, even abusive behavior actually *invites* the other person to continue the behavior. The less you react to provocation, the more provocation you will invite.

EXERCISE: RECOGNIZE THE DAMAGE

Make a list of the ways you have hurt yourself and others by suppressing or repressing your anger.

Remedy #8: Try On a New Way of Dealing with Anger

Without your anger, you may have lost your voice, your motivation, and your courage to get the things you need and deserve. Anger is energy, a motivating force that can empower you to feel less helpless. By releasing it, you will find that you rid yourself of the physical and emotional tension that has sapped your energy—energy that you could otherwise use to motivate yourself to change. Anger can motivate you to set and keep boundaries with the people in your life. The more you express your anger, the less afraid of it you will be. Anger can be your way out. Take it.

- For the next week, practice doing the opposite of what you would normally do when you become angry. For example, if you usually hold your anger in, try letting it out. It may seem uncomfortable or even frightening, but try doing it a little at a time. If someone is inconsiderate or rude to you, risk telling him or her how it made you feel or that you didn't appreciate being treated that way. If you tend to talk yourself out of your anger by telling yourself that you don't want to make waves, try telling yourself instead that it is okay to make waves sometimes and risk letting people know how you really feel.

- Pay attention to how you feel each time you practice this new way of dealing with your anger. Although it will undoubtedly be uncomfortable initially, notice what other feelings come up as you try on this new anger style. For example, those women who practice letting their anger out often discover that they feel energized by the process or that they feel more confident and self-assured. On the other hand, some feel guilty about expressing their anger and feel worse about themselves.

- Keep a log or diary of each time you try on another anger style. In addition to recording the incident, record your feelings surrounding the incident and the end result.

- Even if it is uncomfortable, continue practicing your new style for at least a week. Take small risks at first and then venture out to take even larger risks. For example, if you tend to have a passive anger style, you may start by letting a rude acquaintance know you don't appreciate how he or she treated you. This may make you feel so empowered that you are willing to tell a co-worker that you don't want to be treated a certain way. By the end of the week, perhaps you will be ready to tell your husband when you are angry with him.

There is much more to learn about anger than I can include in this chapter. If anger is a major issue for you, I encourage you to read my book *Honor Your Anger: How Transforming Your Anger Style Can Change Your Life*. In it, you will learn more about anger styles, how to change your anger style into a more healthy one, and how to handle other people's anger.

11

Learn How to Handle Conflict

> The problem is not that there are problems. The
> problem is expecting otherwise and thinking that
> having problems is a problem.
>
> —THEODORE RUBIN

False belief: It is better to avoid conflict at all costs.

Empowering belief: Conflict is a part of life and can be an
opportunity for greater intimacy.

> *This chapter is beneficial for*
> *all types of Nice Girls*

In this chapter, I will discuss yet another phenomenon that
influences women's inability to express their anger and stand up
for themselves. Women and girls have a lot of difficulties with
conflict. Most are uncomfortable with it, and many are afraid of it.
This is due partly to both cultural conditioning and biological predisposition.

In extensive interviews with adults, sociologist Anne Campbell
found that whereas men viewed aggression as a means to control
their environment and integrity, women believed it would terminate
their relationships. In her book *Odd Girl Out*, Rachel Simmons
found the same attitudes in her conversations with girls. The girls
expressed fear that even everyday acts of conflict, not to mention

aggressive outbursts, would result in the loss of the people they cared most about. They therefore refused to engage in even the most basic acts of conflict. To them, conflict equaled loss. Due to this reasoning, the average woman is more willing to compromise her beliefs, values, and desires to maintain a relationship than the average man. Add this to the fact that females are biologically hard-wired to focus on connection and consensus, and we can see why they have so much trouble with conflict. But unless women become better at dealing with conflict, we will continue to lose ourselves in relationships, be dominated by abusive men, and put up with unacceptable behavior.

And there is another negative consequence to women's avoidance of conflict. Because we avoid conflict, we don't have the opportunity to resolve issues. Our natural tendency to value connection over confrontation also often causes women to go underground with their aggression. The truth is that not all Nice Girls are nice. In fact, many are catty, bitchy, and even cruel—all behind the backs of those whom they pretend to like and agree with. They pretend to like someone when they actually dislike the person. They often appear to be so accepting that others feel comfortable confiding in them. But as accepting as some Nice Girls appear to be, they are often actually very critical and judgmental once they gain that confidence.

My mother was a Nice Girl. She was very charming and seemingly agreeable, and people felt instantly comfortable with her. Yet she was extremely critical of them behind their backs. If someone came over to visit she was extremely nice to her, nodding her head in agreement when the person spoke, laughing out loud at her jokes. But once the person left, my mother would criticize her mercilessly. One women friend in particular used to come by unannounced. She would always say something like, "Oh, I'm probably keeping you from something; I should be going," at the beginning of the conversation. Instead of admitting to her that yes, in fact, this visitor was interrupting something, my mother would graciously say, "No, no, please stay. I'm enjoying your company so much!" Yet as soon as the woman left she would complain, "I thought she'd never leave. My God, that woman can talk. I wish she'd stop coming by like that."

Childhood Experiences and Conflict

Although everyone has some conflict in his or her family, not all people express their conflicting feelings openly. Some erupt in a rage; others silently seethe, refusing to even acknowledge conflict. In a typical dysfunctional family, there is either too much or too little conflict. When there is too little conflict, everything is kept hidden. Problems and issues are never fully discussed, and no one ever fights. Unfortunately, when people avoid conflict, the tension between them builds.

On the other hand, when there is too much conflict, there is often emotional or physical abuse. The atmosphere is tense, and the children never know when the next explosion will occur. Fighting becomes a way of life. Children become hypervigilant in anticipating the next attack.

Those raised in families where there was a lot of conflict, anger, or violence often grow up to be afraid of conflict and what they fear it might lead to. This fear of conflict can create very unhealthy ways of behaving. It can cause women to put up with inappropriate, even abusive behavior to the point that they endanger themselves and their children.

One of the most extreme examples of how avoidance of conflict can create a dangerous situation is the case of my client Sedona. Sedona came to see me at the request of her parents, who were at their wit's end about how to protect her. Sedona had been hounded and eventually stalked by a man for nearly five years. This had culminated in his holding her against her will in her apartment until her parents called the police to rescue her.

It all started when Sedona met the man at a party. The man, who I will call Carl, approached her and starting talking to her. Even though Sedona wasn't attracted to him, she didn't want to hurt his feelings, so she was polite. They talked briefly and then she excused herself and went into another room. But the man didn't seem to take the hint. Later on in the evening, he approached her again and asked her out on a date. Again, not wanting to bruise his ego, she made an excuse, telling him that she was too busy to date. Not taking no for an answer, Carl said that since she had to eat, perhaps they could go out to lunch sometime—not a date, just lunch. Sedona didn't know what to say to that, so she reluctantly agreed, just to get him to leave her alone. She had no intention of actually going through with it. She left the party early to get away from him, without giving him her number.

About two days later, she was surprised to find Carl on her doorstep when she came home from work. A little frightened, she asked him how he had found out where she lived. He didn't give her an answer but explained that she had left the party without giving him her number, so he couldn't call her to set up their lunch. Once again, in her attempt to avoid conflict, Sedona now gave Carl her phone number, thinking that when he called she'd just say she was too busy.

That evening, Carl called to set up their lunch. Sedona told him she was busy all week. Carl said he'd call her the next week. Of course, he did call and once again Sedona wasn't direct about not wanting to see him. She again tried to make an excuse, but this time Carl wasn't having it. He confronted her, saying that she was just leading him on, that she was like every other woman he knew. Sedona didn't like being seen in such a negative light and told Carl that she hadn't intended to lead him on. He said he thought she was different, that he thought she was a good and honest person. Sedona assured him that, in fact, she was a good person and tried to be honest. Carl challenged her by saying, "Okay, then, prove it. You promised we could go to lunch, so if you aren't a liar, keep your promise." Sedona took the bait—she did, after all, see herself as someone who kept her promises. By this time, she had begun to feel a little afraid of Carl. Since he knew where she lived, she was concerned that he might show up at her doorstep again. She finally broke down and agreed to have lunch with him the following day.

This was just the beginning of a tumultuous relationship between the two. Sedona explained to me that she was never really interested in Carl but just couldn't seem to get rid of him. She continually tried to appease him by doing as he asked, hoping that it would satisfy him and he'd stop pressuring her. For example, he hounded her for weeks to let him kiss her. She tried explaining to him that she wasn't attracted to him physically and therefore didn't want to kiss him in a romantic way. But Carl was very good with words. He told her, "How do you know you won't start feeling attracted to me once you kiss me? You're not giving it a chance. Kiss me just one time, and if you don't like it, I'll never ask you for another kiss." As Sedona told me, "His arguments always seemed to make sense to me at the time. I'd always think to myself, 'What do I have to lose with just one date, or one kiss, et cetera?' I know it doesn't make sense now, but at the time, somehow it did."

Before Sedona knew it, she was in a relationship with Carl, including having sex with him. "I guess I gradually came to think of him as a friend in some weird kind of way, but I was always pushing him away and he was always pushing for more. I always thought that I could avoid an argument with him if I just agreed to what he wanted and this worked in the moment. But he was never satisfied. He always wanted more."

As time went by, Sedona felt more and more trapped by the relationship with Carl. She finally told a friend about him and her friend told her that Carl sounded like a stalker to her. This surprised Sedona. She always thought stalkers were dangerous people who watched and followed strangers. She didn't think of Carl as a dangerous person—just a persistent one.

By the time the incident occurred that finally brought Sedona into therapy, she was beginning to come out of denial about the fact that Carl had indeed stalked her and just how dangerous he really was. She told me how the incident of being trapped in her apartment had occurred. "I had tried to break it off with Carl many times, but each time it ended up in a big fight with him screaming and yelling at me and causing the neighbors to complain. I didn't want to be kicked out of my apartment so I always agreed to go back with him just to keep him quiet. The last time this happened, I decided I'd break up with him in a letter. That way he wouldn't have a chance to argue with me in person. But I underestimated him. He came over to my apartment in the middle of the night, begging for me to let him in. He said he just wanted to talk and that if I still wanted to break up, he'd leave. I told him no, I wasn't letting him in—I really meant it this time and I wanted him to go away. He started yelling at the top of his lungs that he couldn't make it without me, that he was going to kill himself. That scared me, and I was afraid the neighbors were going to complain to the owner, so I gave in and let him in."

Letting Carl in was a major mistake. He refused to leave, and the next day, when Sedona started getting ready for work, he held her down on the bed and refused to let her get up. He told her she needed to take the day off, that she was tired and stressed and that she looked terrible. She gave in and called her office.

Carl held her in her apartment for three days, constantly trying to talk her into not breaking up with him. Sedona even tried giving in to him and pretending that she had changed her mind and wanted to be back with him, but this time Carl wasn't buying it. Sedona began to fear for her life. Fortunately, her parents, worried when she didn't call them back for three days, called the police.

Although Sedona began seeing me mostly at the urging of her parents, she did tell me during our first session that she wanted to know why she was so passive and why she wasn't more angry at Carl. I started by asking her some questions about her parents. It turned out that they were both very overbearing, and she had grown up in a household where there were a lot of arguments. "I let people get away with a lot because I hate arguments. I didn't ever want to be like my parents, who argued all the time. I wanted to be reasonable. But Carl could talk circles around me."

Bingo. It wasn't much of a mystery after all. Helping Sedona to believe that it is okay to be confrontational and/or angry was going to be more difficult. I started by encouraging her to stand up to her parents. While it was understandable that they were now afraid for her safety, she still needed to assert herself about her right to make her own decisions. She also needed to insist that they respect her personal boundaries.

Even before the Carl situation, Sedona's parents had been overly protective of her. During one of our sessions, she made an important connection. "You know, my parents are just like Carl. They treat me like I'm five years old."

After we met for a few more times, a lot more came out, such as the fact that Sedona's mother was very suffocating. As Sedona explained, "She calls me several times a day to ask me, 'What are you doing?' 'Who is with you?' Sedona realized that when Carl treated her the same way, it simply felt familiar.

Sedona was actually afraid of Carl from the beginning, but she was so used to placating her mother to avoid her wrath that she took on this coping strategy with Carl. Unfortunately, Carl was as controlling as her mother. He went through Sedona's e-mails, and if she didn't answer her phone, he called around looking for her. These were the same types of behaviors she had experienced with her mother.

We also needed to explore why Sedona had let things get so out of hand. We started by reviewing what she told herself each time Carl was too controlling or over the top. First she would tell herself, "It's not that bad." Then she would reason with herself that she didn't want to get him in trouble. But the thing she told herself most often was, "He could get more angry" (meaning violent).

This was at the core of Sedona's fear of conflict—the fear that if she stood up to Carl he would become physically violent with her. Although her parents had never become violent with her or with each other, the threat had always been there.

Although you may have never experienced a situation as extreme as what happened to Sedona, most women need to learn how to handle conflict in healthier ways. Because girls are socialized away from aggression and expected to have perfect relationships, they are often unprepared to negotiate conflict. The information and strategies in the following remedies will help you feel more confident when it comes to dealing with conflicts, whether they are with your partners, your friends, or your family.

Remedies

Remedy #1: Determine Whether Your Avoidance of Conflict Is Mostly Cultural, Familial, or Experiential

Few of us learned effective conflict resolution skills when we were growing up. In fact, those who come from dysfunctional homes learn unhealthy ways of resolving conflict. The following questions will help you explore what lessons you learned from your parents about solving conflicts.

Questionnaire: How Did Your Parents Deal with Conflict?

1. Did your parents discuss problems rationally, or did they blow up at each other?

2. Did they express emotions easily, or did they hold in their feelings?

3. Did your parents tend to blame each other for their problems?

4. Did your parents argue often?

5. Did your parents give each other the silent treatment?

6. Did they yell at each other?

7. Did your parents punish each other?

8. Did they emotionally abuse each other?

Think about the lessons you learned from observing your parents behave in any of these ways. Write your feelings about this in your journal.

Remedy #2: Begin to View Conflict in a Different Way

Conflict-free relationships simply do not exist. In fact, no relationship can survive without conflict. Think about how many relationships you have walked away from in your life because you were unwilling to tell the person how you felt and to work through the problems. Women and girls have a tendency to alienate those they have conflicts with instead of even trying to work those conflicts through. Knowing that conflicts are periodic and that relationships survive them may help you to walk away less often and to engage in repression or passive-aggressive tactics less often.

Conflict cannot be avoided. It is a natural by-product of every relationship. Indeed, conflict *should* not be avoided since it can inspire more effective communication and greater intimacy. It can lead to better understanding between you and the other person. Current research shows that couples who openly disagree or argue actually stay together longer. Conflict does not have to equal loss, as many Nice Girls have been led to believe. On the contrary, it can equal gain. Once you understand this, really understand it, not just intellectually but emotionally, you will stop viewing conflict as a violation of a relationship, and you will no longer be controlled by the fear of loss.

Remedy #3: Create a Positive and Powerful Statement about Conflict

Once again, follow the instructions in chapter 4 to create your positive and powerful statement.

Remedy #4: Stop Thinking That if You Love Someone You Need to Agree with Him or Her

Many people react to conflict by thinking, "If only you loved me, you'd agree with me." You may have experienced this attitude with your past or present partner. But we can't simply wish conflict away. This kind of immature and wishful thinking tends to escalate conflicts instead of resolving them. It also denies another person's right to differ from you, essentially sending the message, "If you really love me, you have to think, feel, and be exactly like me." It places all responsibility for resolving disagreements—and all power to change—in the hands of the other person.

Start by recognizing that conflict is essential to each person's growth and that each relationship inevitably involves a clash of needs, opinions, and feelings. Conflict creates energy, or creative tension, which encourages relationships to grow and evolve. When a relationship is disrupted by conflicting needs or events, when it is filled with creative tension, it pushes each person to "figure it out." Creative tension prods seemingly opposite or out of sync people to dance together until they learn from each other and become harmonious.

Remedy #5: Begin to Believe That Not All Differences Are Irreconcilable

The next step is to recognize that, contrary to what you may have learned growing up, not all differences are irreconcilable and not all conflicts are unsolvable. Most conflicts can be resolved amicably if both people are willing to communicate and work toward that end. If you keep these things in mind, you won't be afraid to disagree with your partner or family member.

Of course, resolving conflicts also requires that both parties or family members commit to working out problems instead of falling back on old standbys such as taking sides in an argument, gossiping and backbiting, name-calling, storming off in anger, or silently seething in anger and refusing to talk to each other. If you are a positive role model for more constructive problem solving, you will have a positive impact on your relationship or your family.

Remedy #6: Let Go of Your Either/Or, Black-and-White Thinking.

If you stubbornly try to force another person to change, or to prove that you are right and he or she is wrong, reconciliation becomes impossible. But if you approach conflict with the goal of coming together, resolution is not only possible but probable. This will require that you let go of the kind of black-and-white thinking that insists there is only one answer or one way of looking at things. It is important to recognize that there are lots of gray areas—seldom is one point of view completely true and another completely false. Both parties can have valid points of view—there doesn't have to be a winner.

Remedy #7: Learn "Fair Fighting" Techniques

The more vulnerable we feel and the more dependent we are on someone, the more power they have to hurt us and, in turn, to anger us. Given the fact that anger is inevitable in relationships, it is vital that we learn the best ways to air our differences. In fact, the long-term success of any relationship depends greatly on the couple's discovering appropriate avenues for expressing and dealing with each other's anger.

Having the ability to freely express anger with each other is a sign of a solid, healthy relationship. Relationships in which one or both partners are unable to acknowledge their own anger or listen to the anger of the other partner tend to be fragile and stilted as opposed to strong and spontaneous. Neither partner may have the confidence that the relationship can withstand the expression of anger.

Instead of fearing anger, set ground rules that both you and the other person can live with. This will help you to begin on equal footing psychologically. You can create your own ground rules, but I suggest they include the following basic assumptions:

1. We will take turns hearing each other out.

2. We will respect each other's position.

3. We understand that each person has a right to his or her own opinion, feelings, and position.

4. We will do our best to find a solution to our problem and the source of our anger.

5. We both agree that there will be no blaming, personal attacks, low blows, or intimidation.

6. There will be no manipulation, diversionary ploys, or exploitative tactics.

Make a point of talking to the person you are upset with as soon as possible. The less time that elapses, the more productive your conversation will be. Conversely, the longer the time between your being hurt and your expressing it to the other person, the more problematic the conflict becomes.

That being said, give yourself time to cool off before confronting your partner. Schedule a time when both of you will be free to talk without being distracted or interrupted.

Sometimes we just need to hash things out with each other. Each person needs to have an opportunity to voice his or her feelings and to know that his or her partner has really heard his or her point of view. The following are instructions for having a fair fight, one that does not escalate into emotional abuse or physical violence:

1. Make sure you will not be interrupted (turn off the phone and the TV, wait until the kids are asleep), allowing yourselves at least half an hour of undivided attention.

2. Don't have a fight if either of you has been drinking or taking drugs.

3. Know what it is you are fighting about and stick to one issue at a time.

4. Clearly describe the problem behavior. Do not attack the other person.

5. Describe how the problem affects you or your feelings.

6. Do not bring up past problems; stay in the present.

7. Don't tell the other person how he or she thinks or feels or should think or feel.

8. Don't threaten or bribe.

9. Ask for feedback.

10. Don't bring in third parties.

11. Do not resort to name-calling, insults, or other forms of verbal abuse.

12. Humor is okay, but don't ridicule the other person.

13. Don't destroy things, especially things that are meaningful to the other person.

14. There is never an excuse for hitting, slapping, or any other form of physical abuse.

15. Take a time-out if tension is mounting.

16. Balance the negative with something positive. Say positive things about the problem or the other person.

17. Try to settle things, at least temporarily, in thirty minutes.

18. Work out a flexible solution or compromise.

19. Realize that the decision is not permanent. You can renegotiate.

20. Commit to following through.

21. Actively work toward a solution.

22. Seek counseling if you're unable to resolve the conflict.

Remedy #8: Learn Nonviolent Communication

Nonviolent communication (or NVC) is a technique that uses language and communication skills to guide us in reframing how we express ourselves and hear others. Created by Marshall B. Rosenberg, PhD, the founder and director of educational services for the Center for Nonviolent Communication, NVC teaches us to express ourselves with honesty and clarity, while simultaneously paying attention to others in a respectful and empathetic way. This leads us to hearing our own deeper needs as well as those of others.

Participants learn to identify and clearly articulate what they concretely want in a given situation. The form is a simple yet powerful one. Resistance, defensiveness, and violent reactions are minimized. Through its emphasis on deep listening—to ourselves as well as others—NVC fosters respect, attentiveness, and empathy.

There are four components to the NVC model:

1. *Observation.* We observe the concrete actions of others that are affecting our well-being.

2. *Feeling.* We state how we feel when we observe this action: we are hurt, scared, joyful, amused, irritated. The trick is to be able to articulate this observation without introducing any judgment or evaluation—to simply say what it is that people are doing, which we either like or don't like.

3. *Needs.* We say what needs of ours are connected to the feelings we have identified.

4. *Specific request.* We communicate the concrete actions we desire so as to enrich our lives.

As you can see, this formula takes you deeper than merely communicating assertively. It fosters compassion between people and helps resolve conflicts in a positive way.

The use of NVC does not require that the people with whom we are communicating be literate in NVC or even motivated to relate to us compassionately. If you stay with the principles, motivated solely to give and receive compassionately, and do everything you can to let others know this is your only motive, they will join you in the process and eventually you will be able to respond compassionately to one another. This may not happen quickly, but compassion inevitably blossoms.

There is much more to NVC than I have briefly outlined here. Rosenberg has written a book titled *Nonviolent Communication: A Language of Life*, and NVC courses are offered internationally. For more information go to www.cnvc.org.

12

Start Facing the Truth about People

> You never know what is enough unless you know
> what is more than enough.
>
> —William Blake

False belief: There is good in everyone, and if you give someone enough chances, he or she will eventually show you his or her good side.

Empowering belief: It is more important to take care of my emotional and physical well-being than it is to give someone a second chance.

> *This chapter is especially beneficial for
> Innocents, Martyrs, Enlightened Ones*

Often, women give second and third chances for the same reason they insist on being fair—because girls and women are expected to be patient and compassionate. Others give second chances because they were not given a second chance themselves.

The concept of giving someone a second chance is a good one. After all, we all make mistakes. Unfortunately, sometimes giving someone a second chance means we are giving the person another opportunity to hurt us, betray us, or take advantage of us. Those with abusive personalities actually view a second chance as a sign that you are a pushover and will not stand up for yourself in the future. For this kind of person, a second chance is an open invitation to do it again.

When One More Chance Is One Too Many

Women, especially those who have been emotionally, physically, or sexually abused, give people too many chances. While the healthy response to abusive behavior is to feel self-protective, even to the point of deciding to stay away from the person, women who have been victimized tend to make excuses for the abusive person's behavior and convince themselves that either the abuse was their own fault, or the person was just stressed out and will never do it again.

In this chapter, I will encourage you to stop making excuses for men and women who behave badly. This includes people who are abusive, those who treat you with disrespect, partners who are unable to make a commitment, and partners who cheat on you. By making excuses for and tolerating these behaviors, women are giving others permission to continue to use and abuse them.

As difficult as it is to recognize, there are people who have no conscience, who may use a woman's natural tendency to be compassionate against her or who will work at getting a woman to pity them as a way of taking further advantage of her. Although pity and sympathy are forces for good when they are reactions to deserving people who have made a mistake, when these feelings are wrestled out of us by the undeserving, by people whose behavior is consistently abusive or antisocial, we are being manipulated. The most powerful example is the battered wife whose abusive husband beats her routinely and then sits at the kitchen table, head in his hands, moaning that he cannot control himself and begging for forgiveness.

In addition to confronting the false belief that everyone has good in them that we can pull out if we are patient enough, in this chapter I will expose similar forms of erroneous thinking, such as "You can affect other people's behavior by behaving in certain ways yourself" and "If you treat other people the way you'd like to be treated, they'll eventually catch on."

Carol had been married to her husband Cliff for ten years. During that time, he gambled most of her money away and cheated on her several times. He always promised he would stop gambling, but, of course, he didn't. He promised he would stop cheating, but she knew he hadn't. Then one day, Cliff told Carol that he had fallen in love with a woman at work and was leaving Carol to be with her. Carol was devastated. She cried for over a month, barely making it to work every day.

Fast forward six months. Cliff called Carol to tell her he had made a huge mistake. He didn't love the other woman after all—he loved Carol. Could he please come back?

Carol's pride had been hurt when Cliff left her for someone else and so she was reluctant to take him back. Even though she still loved him, she had begun to pick up the pieces of her life (emotionally and financially). But Cliff told her that he was different now. He told her that he was ashamed of how he had treated her and that he had started going to church. He began crying on the phone and begged her to at least agree to see him one more time.

Carol didn't want to be cruel, so she agreed to meet him. What she saw surprised her greatly. Her husband looked emaciated. He'd lost weight and his eyes had dark circles around them. Her heart went out to him. After all, she later told me, he had been her husband for a long time. She didn't want to see him suffering so.

Cliff explained to Carol that he had been on a destructive path his whole life. Now, he said, he had finally hit bottom and was determined to change. He had been talking to the pastor of the church he had been going to and felt he'd found the answers he had been searching for. Then he begged Carol to take him back and give him one more chance. "Don't throw me away," he cried. Then he got down on his knees and told her that he loved her, that he had always loved her. Would she please give him another chance?

Carol's heart melted when Cliff declared his love for her. "After all, everyone deserves another chance. I felt so sorry for him when he begged me not to 'throw him away' because that is how he felt as a child, like his parents had thrown him away." When I pointed out to her that she had already given him many, many chances she countered with, "Yes, but he had never gone to church before. He really did seem like a different person."

Carol agreed to "date" Cliff and see how things went. Two months passed, and Cliff continued to go to church. He even talked Carol into going as well, and they both sought counsel from the pastor. "Cliff seemed to be really trying. He read the Bible every day. I wanted so desperately to believe that he had really changed. I had a hard time trusting him, and I talked about this with the pastor. He told me that I needed to forgive Cliff for his past sins and support him now in his new life. And so I finally gave in and had him move back into the house."

Within a month, Cliff was back to his old ways. It started gradually at first. He made excuses for why he couldn't go to church regularly (he was sick, he had to work, he didn't need it anymore). Then Carol found some scratch-off tickets from the local convenience store in the pocket of his jacket. This was her first hint that he was starting to gamble again. When she confronted him with the tickets, he swore they were old ones and turned the whole thing around, accusing her of being paranoid. "He looked so deeply wounded when I made the accusation, I couldn't help but believe him."

Carol finally stopped believing him when she got their credit card statement at the end of the month. There had been a cash advance of $500 three times that month. She knew in her heart what this meant, but just to make sure, she called the credit card company. Sure enough, the signature on the advances was her husband's.

Carol was crushed, but she also felt something else. "This time I couldn't talk myself out of it. I knew in no uncertain terms that he had once more started gambling and that he would never change. There was nothing he could say this time to convince me to give him another chance. I was done."

Even so, Carol came to see me because she wanted to make sure she didn't weaken. She had kicked Cliff out of the house and filed for divorce, but he called her constantly and sometimes came pounding at the door, begging her for another chance. "I'm not going to take him back, but it is so hard to hear him crying and begging like that. I can't help but feel sorry for him, but now I know that is a trap."

Carol also wanted to make sure she didn't make the same mistake again and get involved with someone else with similar problems. This, of course, meant that we needed to explore Carol's background to discover why she was so susceptible to giving second chances. As it turned out, Carol's mother had always made excuses for her alcoholic husband's behavior, no matter how inappropriate. When he was so drunk that he stumbled and fell, Carol's mother would say, "He's just tired from working so hard." When he lost his job because of his drinking, her mother explained, "His boss had it in for him."

Making the connection between her mother's behavior and her own helped Carol tremendously. This is what she shared with me during one of our sessions: "I've thought about this a lot. The fact that my mother gave my father so many chances and made so many excuses for him didn't help anyone. It didn't help my father, who just kept on drinking. In fact, it probably enabled him to continue drinking. And it certainly didn't help my mother or myself. After my father lost his job, he never got another one. He did odd jobs now and then, but mostly my mother ended up supporting us. This realization has made me think about giving second chances in a whole new way."

I'm happy to report that I recently heard from Carol, who proudly told me that she had not allowed Cliff to return. She was now involved with a man who treats her with respect and consideration. "So far, he hasn't done anything that I have to overlook or make excuses for. But if he does, I'm no longer afraid I'll give too many chances. My new motto is: 'You get one chance with me—so you better use it well.'"

Why It Is Particularly Important to Not Give Abusers Second Chances

You've no doubt heard this before, but it bears repeating. Once a man (or a woman) becomes physically abusive, he is very likely to repeat the behavior. In fact, evidence shows that once a man has crossed the line into physical abuse, his behavior usually escalates. This means that if he pushed you once, the next time he is likely to push you harder or hit you. If he slapped you in the face, he is likely to sock you with a clenched fist the next time. For this reason primarily, it is important *not* to give second chances when it comes to someone's physically abusing you.

Another important reason not to give such a person a second chance is that many abusers interpret this as permission to continue abusing you. Most abusers don't stand up to men or those who are their physical equal. Instead, they pick on women and those who are weaker. They are actually looking for someone to bully and control.

If you give an abuser a second chance, this essentially tells the person he or she has found a willing victim.

Abusers tend to lose respect for anyone who allows herself to be mistreated. This includes those who allow emotional abuse as well as physical abuse. In essence, your giving an abuser a second chance may actually cause him or her to respect you *less*, and this in itself may give the person permission to abuse you further.

Many of you reading this book have already heard this information before. And yet in spite of this, many women remain in relationships with abusive partners. Many continue giving their abusive partners another chance. In fact, recent statistics tell us that the average abused woman goes back to her abuser *seven* times. Why do they do this? The main reason is that women feel compelled to "work things out" with their partners. We are biologically and culturally programmed to be peacemakers.

Remedies

Remedy #1: Learn the Difference between Having the Blind Trust of a Child and Becoming Discerning—between Judging Someone and Protecting Yourself

This is an important transition to make. If someone hurts, offends, or betrays you, it should be a warning to you that this person is capable of doing it again. This doesn't mean that you must end the relationship and not give the person a second chance, but it does mean that you can no longer be completely trusting of the person—at least until he or she proves herself to you once again. One of the wonderful things about children is that they forgive and forget so easily and so completely. But unfortunately, this also puts children at greater risk of being repeatedly used or abused by uncaring adults.

You are no longer a child, and you can no longer afford to excuse someone for disappointing or hurting you because he or she asks you to or expects you to. You don't have to judge the person too harshly—we all make mistakes. But on the other hand, only a fool (or a child) pretends that it never happened. This is where discernment comes in. Discerning adults take into consideration a person's past behavior and use it to determine how safe they are with this person. They may feel safe enough to risk some interactions, while not feeling safe enough to risk others. For example, a discerning woman would not leave her husband alone with an attractive girl-friend if he has cheated on her in the past. A discerning woman would not leave the liquor cabinet unlocked when she leaves the house if she knows that her teenage son has taken liquor from it before.

Remedy #2: Stop Blaming Yourself

One of the main reasons Nice Girls give second chances is that they often take too much responsibility for the actions of others. Instead of getting angry at someone for behaving inconsiderately, inappropriately, or even abusively, they often try to put themselves in the other person's place and become "understanding." And Nice Girls often go one step further—they often blame themselves for the actions of others.

Holly had been raised to always think about another person's feelings before her own. When she came home from school and told her mother about being bullied by another child, instead of comforting her, her mother would say, "What did you do to make her angry? People don't just hit you for no reason." When Holly replied that she'd done nothing, her mother didn't believe her. "People always have a good reason for their behavior," she would be told. "If you just put yourself in their place you'll understand and you won't ever have to get angry."

While Holly's mother may have had good intentions concerning teaching her daughter empathy, her attempts were convoluted and extremely negating of Holly's feelings—so much so that as an adult, Holly is unaware of what she is feeling at any given time. Worst of all, her mother taught her to blame herself if someone treats her badly.

Remedy #3: Differentiate between Offenses and People Who Warrant a Second Chance and Those Who Do Not

If a friend or a lover is late to meet you for lunch or forgets your birthday, it's probably okay to give him or her a second chance. But more serious offenses, such as being unfaithful, getting drunk and becoming abusive, or maliciously starting a terrible rumor about you, probably do not deserve another chance.

Some people deserve a second chance more than others. These include:

- Those who have been understanding, compassionate, and forgiving toward you
- Those who generally treat you with consideration, kindness, and respect
- Those who have genuinely apologized and taken responsibility for their offensive behavior

What is a genuine apology? A genuine, or meaningful, apology is one that communicates what I call the three R's—regret, responsibility, and remedy. The following information is an adaptation of material from my book *The Power of Apology*:

1. A statement of *regret*. This should include an expression of empathy toward you, including an acknowledgement of the inconvenience, hurt, or damage that the person caused you.

2. An acceptance of *responsibility* for his or her actions. This means not blaming anyone else for what he or she did and not making excuses for his or her actions, but instead taking full responsibility for what he or she did and for the consequences of his or her actions.

3. A statement of the person's willingness to take some action to *remedy* the situation. This can be a promise to not repeat the offensive action, to work toward not making the same mistake (by going to therapy, or joining a 12-step program), or by making restitution for the damages he or she caused.

Unless all three of these elements are present, most people have a sense that something is missing in the apology and will feel short-changed. They will also not feel safe enough to give the other person another chance.

Remedy #4: Don't Allow Anyone to Pressure You to Forgive Him or Her if You Are Not Ready

Each person needs to come to forgiveness on his or her own, not be pressured to forgive because it is the politically correct thing to do. As wise as spiritual leaders, philosophers, and therapists are concerning the importance of forgiveness, sometimes forgiveness is not possible—or even recommended. Unfortunately, because of the focus on forgiveness within the religious, 12-step, and even psychological communities, we have not been given permission to choose not to forgive. Contrary to popular belief, forgiveness is not necessary for healing, and, in some cases, it is not necessarily the healthiest thing to do. This is especially true when forgiving is tantamount to giving someone permission to hurt you again.

Sometimes we need to hold on to our anger to cope and survive. This is especially true for those who have been victimized. Anger can help us rise above the victimization and fight our way back from the most devastating of traumas. For example, many survivors of sexual abuse need their anger to help them feel separate from their abuser (victims of child sexual abuse often feel particularly, inextricably enmeshed with their perpetrator, especially if he or she was a parent or a sibling). They need their anger to help ward off the overwhelming shame and guilt that constantly floods over them (victims of all forms of childhood abuse, especially victims of sexual abuse, tend to blame themselves for the abuse).

Sometimes our resistance to forgiving is telling us something important, and instead of trying to get past our resistance, we need to honor it. Even though someone apologizes, it does not necessarily mean that we must forgive him or her. In some situations, such as when the person apologizing is a repeat offender, forgiving is impossible because there seems to be no hope for change.

This was the case with Claudia. Shortly after she got married, her husband, Max, began to physically abuse her. After every incident of abuse, he would begin to cry and plead with her to forgive him: "I'm sorry, Claudia. Please forgive me. I didn't mean to. You just make me so mad. I promise I won't ever do it again."

Each time Max apologized, Claudia forgave him. Even though what he had done had devastated her, he seemed so pitiful and so sincere in his apologies that not forgiving him seemed like a heartless thing to do. She loved him dearly and wanted to believe he was genuinely sorry. But before long, he was punching her and pushing her around the room all over again.

It took two years of this before Claudia finally came to the painful conclusion that Max was never going to change. He'd promised to go to therapy many times but each time had backed out at the last minute. Sometimes he'd manage to go months without abusing her, giving her false hope that perhaps this time things really were going to be different. Then, after two years of this repetitive cycle, one day something changed inside Claudia. "He came into our bedroom about an hour after beating me, looking sheepish, as usual. He proceeded to say he was sorry, that he didn't know what came over him, that he was going to get some help, that he loved me. But this time it just didn't work. I wasn't touched by the pain in his voice as I had always been in the past. And I wasn't moved by his apologies. I'd always believed that he really couldn't help himself, and so I always believed he really was sorry. But suddenly I questioned his sincerity. It all sounded phony to me. I was shocked. It felt like I'd been fooled all this time. That he really wasn't sorry at all. That it was just words. Empty words. That was the day I decided I wasn't going to forgive him again. The time for forgiveness was over."

That night, while Max was sleeping, Claudia sneaked out of the house and never returned. That was a year ago. Since that time, she has managed to put her life back together and to resist the temptation to return to him, even though she often feels pulled in that direction.

The last time I saw Claudia, she told me, "It makes me so mad when people tell me I should forgive Max for what he did to me. They have no idea what forgiving him did to me all those years. And they don't understand that I can't afford to forgive him now. If I forgive him, I'm afraid I'll start to make excuses all over again for what he did to me. If I forgive him, I'm afraid I'll weaken and go back to him."

Perhaps with more time and distance, Claudia will be able to forgive her estranged husband. For now, she needs to keep her heart hardened against him. Who can blame her?

Remedy #5: When It Comes to Abuse, Make a Distinction between Second Chances That Are Based on Real Hope for Change and Those That Are Based on False Hope

According to Lundy Bancroft, an expert with many years' experience working with abusive men, there are two main principles to keep in mind when determining how much potential an abuser has to become a respectful, considerate partner:

- He cannot change unless he deals deeply with his entitled and superior attitudes. No superficial changes that he may make offer any real hope for the future.

- It makes no difference how *nice* he is being to you, since almost all abusers have nice periods. What matters is how *respectful* and *noncoercive* he chooses to become.

The following questionnaire, adapted from Bancroft's book *Why Does He Do That? Inside the Minds of Angry and Controlling Men*, will help you identify changes that show promise of being genuine. Answer yes or no to the following questions. We are looking for yes answers.

1. Has he stopped behaviors that are threatening or intimidating?

2. Has he begun to treat your opinions with respect, even when they differ strongly from his?

3. Does he listen without interrupting to your side in arguments? Does he then make a serious effort to respond thoughtfully to your points or concerns, even if he doesn't agree with them?

4. Does he accept your right to express your anger toward him, especially when it involves his history of mistreating you?

5. Are you free to raise your grievances, new or old, without retaliation?

6. Is he responding to your grievances and doing something about them (for example, changing the ways he behaves toward the children)?

7. Has he greatly reduced or eliminated his use of controlling behaviors (such as sarcasm, rolling his eyes, talking over you, and other demonstrations of disrespect or superiority) during conversations and arguments?

8. When he does slip back into controlling behavior, does he take you seriously when you tell him about it, and does he continue working on improving?

9. Does he take into account how his actions affect you without having to be constantly reminded?

10. Is he being noticeably less demanding, selfish, and self-centered?

11. Has he stopped talking about his abuse as if it were something he couldn't help and begun to acknowledge that he used it to control you?

12. Has he stopped blaming you for his abusive behavior?

13. Is he respecting your right to freedom and independence? This includes refraining from all interference with your friendships and giving up the demand to know where you are and whom you are with.

14. Has he stopped making excuses for his treatment of you, including not using your behavior as an excuse for his anger or abusive ways?

15. Is he being respectful about sex, including not pressuring you or engaging in guilt trips?

16. Has he stopped cheating or flirting with other women, or using these or other behaviors to keep you anxious about whether or not he will stray?

17. Is he being fair and responsible about money and finances, including allowing you to keep your own assets in your own name?

18. Has he expanded his contribution to household and child-rearing responsibilities and stopped taking your domestic work for granted or treating you like a servant?

19. Has he begun supporting your strengths instead of striving to undermine them?

20. Has he shown a new willingness to conduct himself nonabusively, even during major arguments?

If you answered no to any of these questions, this is a sign that there is work your partner still needs to do. You have a right to bring up your concerns about his progress, and if he is committed to changing he will listen and take you seriously and acknowledge that he does, indeed, have work to do. According to Bancroft, if he is impatient or critical of you for "not being satisfied" with his changes, it is a sign that his overt abusive behaviors will be coming back before long. Bancroft's experiences with abusive men, as well as my own, have been that many of the small- or medium-level improvements generally slip away over time and that the man who actually maintains his progress is usually the one who changes more completely, even though his progress may be slower.

If your partner is truly on the road to recovery, you will notice a dramatic difference in him. You will feel almost as if you are with a different person. This signals the fact that there has been a real shift in his attitude rather than just the superficial ways that he has used in the past to smooth things over.

If you are considering giving an abusive man another chance, you need to hold him to an even higher standard than you would a nonabusive partner. This means that you don't just let things slide, that you are diligent about watching for signs that he is slipping back into old patterns and behaviors.

Remedy #6: Face the Fact That You Cannot Rehabilitate Anyone

While everyone does indeed have some good in him or her, there do exist people who have buried any semblance of good so deep inside them that it is inaccessible. Women who believe that they can somehow rehabilitate partners who have shown themselves to be cruel, untrustworthy, or without conscience are just fooling themselves. According to Martha Stout, PhD, the author of *The Sociopath Next Door*, the combination of consistently bad behavior with frequent plays for pity are as close to a warning mark on a conscienceless person's forehead as you can get.

In her book, Stout provides what she calls "the rule of three" to help women learn when to stop giving second chances: "One lie, one broken promise, one abusive comment may be a misunderstanding. Two may involve a serious mistake. But three lies says you're dealing with a liar. Cut your losses and get out as soon as you can. Leaving now will be easier and less costly. Do not give your money, your secrets, or your affection to a three-time loser. Your valuable gifts will be wasted."

13

Start Supporting and Protecting Yourself

Something we were withholding made us weak,
Until we found it was ourselves.

—ROBERT FROST

False belief: Women need men to protect and support them financially.

Empowering belief: I am a strong and capable woman. I can take care of and protect myself.

This chapter is especially beneficial for
Doormats, Victims

Earlier in the book, I wrote that women can no longer depend on men to protect them. Most males are no longer raised to think of girls and women as needing their protection and, unfortunately, some boys and men today often have a very negative view of women and are more likely to exploit than to protect them. Yet many girls and women mistakenly believe that they can look to and depend on boys and men for protection. To make matters worse, many women still hold onto the idea that they cannot make it financially without a man.

These false beliefs can be easily explained. Biologically, women are physically weaker than men and, for most of our history, have been dependent on men for protection and security. In spite of the strides we have made, it is still basically a man's world. Women still do not earn as much money as men do for the same jobs (the latest research says that women make approximately 70 percent of what men earn for the same job), and men still dominate most arenas, including business, finance, law, medicine, and politics. Women still have to fight for any advances they make in most professions.

Most women *prefer* to be in a relationship since, as humans, we need others to help us feel connected and to ward off feelings of loneliness and isolation. But no woman *needs* a man to financially support her or to protect her from the big, bad world. We are quite capable of doing these things on our own. If you are one of the many women who still don't quite believe this, I hope this chapter and its remedies section will help you to not only begin to see the light but to shed the limiting beliefs that keep you emotionally and financially dependent on men.

Financial Insecurity

Many women, because their salaries are often still less than men's, continue to enter into relationships partly or primarily for financial security. Many still believe they can't survive without the support of a man, especially if these women have children.

Make no mistake about it. Money is power. Money can be a magnet for women who carry the false belief that they cannot support themselves financially. These women consistently become dependent on the men in their life because they allow themselves to be "bought" and because they tend to turn complete control of their finances over to the man.

That some women may be in a situation where they need financial assistance from time to time is not the problem. The problem is that some women believe they need to placate and cater to a man in order to be taken care of. This is akin to slavery or prostitution. In addition to your needing to understand on an emotional level that you do not need a man to survive, you need to learn to support yourself financially. Those who feel stuck with a man because they are in a financial bind need to learn how to connect with their strengths to break out of the vicious cycle of depending on a man for financial survival.

"I Can't Make It without a Man"

It is surprising how many women still believe that they can't make it without a man. In fact, it is the number-one reason women stay with abusive men. Those who are brutally beaten or verbally abused and humiliated by their husbands or boyfriends will insist that they can't leave because they wouldn't be able to support themselves and their children financially. Many women will also explain that although their husbands are abusive, they do feel protected by them, and the men feel far less dangerous to them than does going out and facing the cruel world.

I met Lily when I was working as the assistant director and head counselor at a battered women's shelter. It was my first paying job since I had obtained my license as a marriage, family, child therapist. I was full of hope and the belief that I could really help abused women. Lily came to the shelter with her two children, ages four and seven. Hers was one of the most extreme cases anyone at the shelter had experienced.

Lily's husband had repeatedly beaten her to the point that she had been hospitalized several times for broken bones. Many social workers had tried to intervene throughout the years, to no avail. Lily refused to admit that her husband beat her. This was before the law was passed that allowed law enforcement officers to file a charge themselves if they suspected a woman was being beaten. So, time after time, her husband would arrive at the hospital with roses, profess his undying love for her, and convince Lily to come home.

The final straw for Lily was when her husband hit her so hard that she became deaf in one ear. The doctor at the hospital told her he was afraid that the next time he saw her, she would be permanently crippled or dead. This seemed to flip a switch in Lily's mind, and she finally admitted to authorities that her husband was a batterer. She agreed to come to the shelter immediately with her two children.

Lily filed a restraining order and agreed to the shelter's policy to never divulge her whereabouts to anyone—not even close friends and family. She seemed to be doing fairly well at the shelter, attending nightly group therapy sessions and seeing me once or twice a week. During our sessions, she was able to express some of her emotions—her fear that she wouldn't be able to make it on her own and her sadness at the ending of her marriage. She cried frequently, telling me about what a wonderful man her husband had been at one time and how he had turned into a monster because of his drinking. She was worried that because she had no skills, she wouldn't be able to find a job and would have to live off welfare the rest of her life. Her husband had made a good living and she didn't want her children to have to grow up poor.

What Lily seemed unable to do was to connect with her feelings of anger toward her husband for terrorizing her the way he did, nor was she able to recognize how damaging it was for her children to have witnessed his abuse of her. She rationalized, saying that he never hit her in front of the children and that she had always made up stories about how she had gotten all the cuts and bruises she so often had. Nevertheless, I felt hopeful that, with the support of so many shelter employees and volunteers, Lily would be able to get past her fears and gain the strength and courage it would take to stay away from her husband.

But my hope turned out to be unwarranted. One night, after being at the shelter for about a month, Lily called her husband from a phone booth down the street. During the course of the conversation, she broke down and told him where she was. That night, she sneaked out of the shelter with her two children and got into his car.

When we discovered that Lily was gone, everyone at the shelter felt devastated—staff and residents alike. I felt horrified and completely discouraged when I realized that Lily would choose to go back to such a monster when she had such a good chance of breaking away.

In a phone call with Lily several days later, she told me that she just didn't believe she could make it on her own. As abusive as her husband could be, she said that she knew he loved her. She knew that as long as she was with him, she and the kids would never go without. For Lily, this was more important than her personal safety or even the emotional well-being of her children.

Lily's is an extreme but far too common example of what can happen when a woman has the belief that she must have a man to survive. As I was to learn time and again during my long career of working with abused women, many women simply do not believe they can make it without a man, and they will put up with anything to achieve a feeling of security.

This belief is unfounded. As difficult as Lily's situation was, had she remained at the shelter she would have received the financial aid she needed until she could complete the training that would enable her to support herself and her children. She would have received the therapy and support she needed to build up her self-esteem, her strength, and her courage.

This is what happened for another shelter client I will call Carrie. Carrie had three children when she came to the shelter. She had not graduated from high school, having had her first child when she was only sixteen. Now Carrie had had enough from her abusive husband. She was determined to save her children from having to witness any further abuse and was going to do anything in her power to get them out.

Carrie ended up staying at the shelter for two months (the limit to how long a woman could stay). During that time, she enrolled in a secretarial course at a local business college. She also saw me every day for counseling. "I need to heal from all this so I can be strong for my kids," she told me. "I don't ever want to be dependent on a man again—ever."

Even though Carrie had been used to a rather affluent lifestyle with her husband, she was willing to exist on welfare, food stamps, and donated items from the shelter until she could find a job. "My pride is not what's important here—I lost that a long time ago when I stayed with my husband after the first time he beat me. What's important now is my safety and the safety of my children, and proving to myself that I can take care of them myself."

That's just what Carrie did. She got a secretarial job about a month after she left the shelter. Even though the salary was low, she stuck with it until she was promoted to a living wage. She also starting selling a health food product popular at the time, and found she was quite a good salesperson. Between the money she made at her full-time job and the commissions she made on her sales, she managed to make a good enough living to support herself and her kids. Within six months of leaving the shelter, she was able to get off welfare and food stamps completely.

Start Protecting Yourself

Not only can women no longer depend on men to protect them, they can't depend on the "kindness of strangers." Neither can they trust that a seemingly nice guy won't harm them. Many potential muggers or rapists often use ploys such as asking for directions, paying a woman a compliment, or appealing to a woman's vanity by asking her if she is a model or an actress. Unfortunately, this means that women have to be suspicious of men who are strangers.

Rape is the secret fear of many women. In a recent survey, two-thirds of American women reported that they don't feel safe, especially when walking alone down a street at night. This fear of sexual assault is not unfounded since it is estimated that 12.1 million American women have been the victim of forcible rape and that 1 out of 8 will be assaulted in her lifetime. But women can do a lot to prevent themselves from being raped, and they can stop expecting other men to protect them and start protecting themselves.

Studies have finally dispelled the myth that women are unable to protect themselves and that resistance will only "make things worse." The latest data shows that immediate and aggressive responses, including fighting back, *are* effective. Conversely, pleading, reasoning, or appealing to a rapist's humanity—all typical Nice Girl tactics—do not work. According to Dr. Judith Herman, in her classic book *Trauma and Recovery*, "The women who fought to the best of their abilities were not only more likely to be successful in thwarting the rape attempt, but less likely to suffer severe distress symptoms. By contrast, women who submitted without struggle were more likely to be highly self-critical and depressed in the aftermath."

The most significant thing you can do to protect yourself from rape is to take a women's self-defense course. Self-defense training will help you with everyday assertiveness and boundary setting, as well as prepare you to fight back if you are physically attacked. Good training programs incorporate an understanding of the kinds of violence most often experienced by women and the common social and psychological barriers women face in learning to fight back. You will gain both physical and verbal defense skills. It is an excellent vehicle for exploring anger, grief, and fear concerning violence against women and for tapping into the joy that can come from finding your voice and discovering your internal power.

In the remedies section, I will outline other ways that women can learn to protect themselves.

Even the Strongest Women Can Become Dependent

Although most women today know that it is not good to be dependent on a man, even the strongest women can sometimes revert to being dependent, given the right circumstances. Even the most ardent feminist might find herself in a situation where she needs (or feels she needs) to compromise to achieve the support and protection of men.

I experienced this firsthand when I was in my early thirties. I had met a woman in Los Angeles who lived outside Florence, Italy, and she invited me to come visit her. This prompted me to plan a month-long trip to England, Ireland, and Europe on my own.

I had a wonderful time in England, Ireland, and France and enjoyed my time visiting my friend in her home near Florence, but by the time I left Italy I became more and more exhausted. It took one long day on the train to reach Switzerland, where I spent the night before traveling on to Amsterdam—my last stop before going home.

That first evening in Amsterdam, I was sitting at an outdoor café having a drink when an attractive and friendly man approached me. He told me his name was Jacob and asked if I was from the United States. I said yes. He told me that he loved Americans and asked if he could please sit down. We started talking, and he offered to take me out that night to show me the nightlife in Amsterdam. Since he seemed to be a nice person, I accepted his offer.

We had a great night together, going from one dance club to another. I drank much too much (I had a drinking problem at the time) but was having so much fun I didn't notice. In the wee hours of the morning Jacob asked me to go home with him. I was attracted to him and feeling good, so I agreed.

I don't remember much about the sex we had because I was so drunk, but I do remember waking up the next day and feeling hung over and wishing I was alone in my hotel room. I didn't feel like having to deal with anyone. But Jacob was so sweet to me that I soon stopped wishing for solitude. He gave me some juice and rubbed my feet and later on fixed me breakfast. It felt good to just relax and let someone take care of me.

Jacob offered to show me around Amsterdam. He suggested I check out of my hotel, to save money. It all sounded like a good idea. I'd had to be on guard during most of my trip, making sure I didn't miss my train connections, keeping a close watch on my purse and luggage, maneuvering around strange cities. Suddenly I felt like I didn't have to worry about anything. I didn't have anyplace to go; I didn't have to focus on where I was or who was around me. I just let Jacob take care of everything.

We had a nice day touring around Amsterdam and returned to his apartment early in the evening. He made me dinner while I rested on the couch. After dinner, Jacob started coming on to me sexually. I wasn't feeling sexual, but unfortunately I slipped back into a very old behavior. I felt I couldn't turn him down since he'd been so nice to me. After all, I'd already had sex with him the night before. How could I get out of it? So I had sex with Jacob again, this time sober.

Unfortunately, I felt absolutely no sexual energy toward him. I just went through the motions. It turned out that Jacob had quite a sexual appetite and was ready to go again within an hour. This time, I managed to gather up enough of myself to put him off. But he kept trying—all night long.

By the next morning, I thought I was going to go out of my mind. I just wanted to get as far away from Jacob as I could get. Once again, he was sweet and accommodating, but I was still angry about how often I had to push him away in the night. I couldn't bear to be around him, and I certainly didn't want him to touch me. When he offered to massage my back, I refused.

I felt stuck. I had checked out of my hotel room and my plane didn't leave until the next day. If this happened to me today (which isn't likely since I wouldn't put myself in that position again) I would have simply called a taxi and left, whether I had a hotel room or not. But I wasn't as emotionally strong then as I am today, and I was exhausted from a very long trip. I simply didn't feel like I had the energy to look for another hotel. Plus, there was another factor that at the time I didn't recognize. I had been sexually abused as a child, and the experience of Jacob's pressuring me for sex had triggered unconscious memories of my abuse experience, which, in essence, rendered me powerless. So I stayed with Jacob another day and another horrible night. The day went well enough. I told him I wasn't feeling well (which I wasn't), and we took it easy, taking a barge tour and a ride in the countryside. That night, I told him I didn't feel like having sex—that I still wasn't feeling well. He became very upset, telling me that it was our last night. He said he'd fallen in love with me and was going to miss me terribly. He even tried to make me feel guilty. But it didn't work. I was feeling so smothered by him that I just couldn't bear his touching me, much less having sex with me.

From this experience I came to understand, albeit in a small way, how those who are kidnapped feel—how they often try to befriend their captors. As much as I had come to feel like I was a prisoner in Jacob's apartment, I still didn't want to make him angry. I felt like I owed him something for being so nice to me. I even believed I needed him to take me to the airport.

When I look back on this experience, I am appalled at my behavior. Not only had I been very reckless with my safety (I didn't know this man at all and was in a foreign country; I could have been raped or worse), but I had become dependent on a man—something I could never have imagined I would ever do again.

Remedies

Remedy #1: Don't Let a Man Buy You

The best way to avoid getting into a situation in which you are financially dependent on a man is to not allow a man to buy you. What I mean by this is that you not fall into the trap of being seduced by favors, gifts, offers of money, cars, or apartments. Certainly this does not mean you don't allow a man to pay for your dinner or take you out for a big night on the town. It doesn't even mean that you don't accept a small gift in the beginning of the relationship—such as flowers. But it does mean you shouldn't go out with a man just because you know he has money—especially if you aren't attracted to him in the first place. It means that you don't accept expensive gifts or favors that set up an obligation from a man at the beginning of the relationship. This establishes a very unhealthy precedent and sends a negative message to the man that you can be bought.

No matter how broke you are or how hard it is to pay your bills each month, going out with or staying with a man you don't really like just because he is rich or has good connections is just not worth it. I can't tell you how many women clients I've had who regret having done this very thing. For example, Maxine started dating Jim right after her divorce came through. She'd met him through some business acquaintances. As she explained to me, "I wasn't really attracted to him, but I knew he had a lot of money. My ex-husband had nearly bankrupted us, and I was bound and determined to never get involved with another man unless he had lots of money and could support me in the manner to which I wanted to become accustomed, if you know what I mean."

Maxine found out that being with a rich man wasn't all it was cracked up to be. "Right away, he seemed to think he owned me. He started telling me who I should hang out with and how I should spend my time. He was being so generous with me, I guess I thought it was worth it. But believe me, it wasn't. Things just got worse and worse. He took me on a very expensive vacation to the Caribbean, which was wonderful, but the whole time it was all about what he wanted to do. He never asked me what I'd like to see or do. Because he was paying, he thought he had the right to have complete control. And it was during this trip that he started demanding sex from me—whether I wanted it or not. One night, I had gone back to the hotel room early because I had a headache. He stayed downstairs, entertaining a group of Europeans. When he came up, well after midnight, he insisted on having sex. I told him I still had a headache but he didn't seem to care. When I still refused, he had the nerve to tell me, 'Look, you either put out or I'll go find another whore who will.'

"He apologized the next day saying that he'd had too much to drink, but I never forgot what he said. I knew that in some way he actually did see me as his whore. It was just downhill from then on. I confess, I still accepted his lavish gifts—it was just so hard to resist. But as time went on, I began to feel more and more like a paid prostitute. And he was demanding more and more for his money—strict obedience, what he called 'total loyalty,' which meant that I could never associate with anyone he deemed unacceptable, and the worst part of all—sex on demand.

"By the time I'd had enough, I'd lost all respect for myself. That's why I'm here. I don't ever want to do that to myself again—I don't care how poor I am."

It is very important that you pay your own way with a man and don't accept favors you cannot repay. This sends the message that you can't be bought and that you are a self-sufficient woman who can't be controlled or dominated. Even if you don't have enough money to pay some of the time, you can reciprocate by cooking him dinner or taking him on a picnic you've prepared.

Even after marriage, you will retain a lot more personal power if you continue to support yourself and contribute to the running of the household.

Remedy #2: Keep Your Finances Somewhat Separate

Unfortunately, as I discussed earlier, many women stay with partners they are unhappy with or those who are abusive just because they don't have enough money to pay their own way or to leave. For this reason, even married women or women who live with their partners need to maintain separate bank accounts with enough savings in it so that they are not dependent on their partners to take care of them.

Many women also feel that even though their partners may have a lot of money, and they may not need to work, they need to make their own money so as to feel independent.

Remedy #3: Learn to Protect Yourself from Rapists and Muggers

If you haven't already done so, I strongly recommend that you take a women's self-defense course. There are many to choose from. In the meantime, the following self-defense principles will enable you to better protect yourself.

1. *Stay aware of people in your surroundings.* Most rapists are more predatory in nature than opportunistic. They will often observe or case a situation in which women might be available and alone. A potential rapist will often look at you far longer than what is considered socially acceptable. He may move when you move. He will stop and look around to check

for witnesses. He will often make several passes by his prey in a sort of dry run, seeing if the victim will react or to get a sense of how the attack might work. For this reason, you need to pay attention to who is looking at you. Has the same person or car passed by you twice? Does someone appear to be moving with you?

2. *Keep your distance.* Many potential rapists actually "test" or "interview" a woman to see if she is a good victim. They test her boundaries to gain proximity and size up her defenses. This can occur in a few seconds or over months, preceded by a simple request for directions or persistent unwanted courting. Criminals, especially rapists and stalkers, are experts at violating boundaries. This is how they think: "If I can get this close, I can move in closer. If I can make her comply with one demand, I can help myself to more." Do not enable this progression of yesses. This is where the information on how to say *no* and on setting boundaries presented earlier in the book will come in handy. Take control and nip the problems in the bud. Learn to draw a line, to say no and mean it.

3. *Recognize an "interview" and know what to do.* The interview often starts out with the man trying to discern whether you are alone. *Never* confirm this to any man. If a man asks you if you are alone in a workplace or home, tell him no. Next, a potential rapist may ask you a series of questions in rapid succession or he may change his questions, depending on your answer. He may also refuse to take no for an answer. This is his attempt to disarm you and test how strong you are. Remain calm and don't become flustered with his changing questions. At the same time that he is asking questions, he may be walking closer to you. If this is the case, back up or walk to another area of the room or street away from him. Do not allow a man to corner you or come into your space. And don't be afraid to say something like, "It's clear that I can't help you. I think you should leave." Don't worry about hurting his feelings. Nice guys don't violate your space or sensibilities by pressuring you or crossing your boundaries.

4. *Stay with people, go to people.* Never get into a car with a strange man. If someone attempts to force you into a car, drop to the

ground to prevent him from carrying you away. Do not walk around a building to an alley or enter an elevator or a stairwell if there is only a man present. Stay where others can see you. If you are in a house or other private location, you need to go to people. Run out of the door to a neighbor's house or climb out of a window. If you are being followed in your car, drive to a diner or a convenience store. Go where the lights are.

5. *Keep a barrier between you and the bad guy.* Keep your doors to your house and your car locked at all times. If someone is after you, use a barrier to block him or use distance to gain time. Stay in your car, if approached there. Keep the windows closed. Carry and use pepper spray. The more difficult you make it for him, the more time it takes him, and that means he might be discovered.

6. *Attract attention.* The first thing a rapist will say to you is, "Don't scream or I'll kill you." What he is really telling you, however, is exactly what will ruin his plan. So go ahead, ruin his plan—scream your head off, blow the horn, kick garbage cans over, make a racket. Yell "Fire!" Although you can't count on others coming to your aid, you want to appeal to his fear of getting caught and make him think that someone could hear you. Don't be embarrassed to make a scene.

7. *Control his hips and his hands.* This is a recommendation made by the Rape Escape program. Controlling his hips will prevent penetration. If you can use your feet on his hips, you can control the distance between the two of you. His hands are the weapons he will use against you to hit, stab, or strangle you, so try to block them or pull them away.

8. *Use your strongest weapons against his most vulnerable areas.* Again, this is a recommendation made by the Rape Escape program. His throat, groin, and knees are your primary targets. Your secondary targets are his eyes, face, throat, and abdomen. Your strongest weapons are your kicks, using the bottom of your feet, your elbows, hammer fists, and palm-heel strikes.

Remedy #4: Continue to Work on Your Tendency to Become Dependent or to Lose Yourself in a Relationship

If you have a tendency to be dependent or to lose yourself in a relationship, I strongly recommend that you read my book *Loving Him without Losing You*. In it, you will find important information and strategies to help you overcome these tendencies and to become the strong, independent woman you were meant to be.

PART THREE

FROM NICE GIRL TO
STRONG WOMAN

14

The Four C's: Developing Confidence, Competence, Conviction, and Courage

> Power can be seen as power with rather than power
> over, and it can be used for competence and co-
> operation, rather than dominance and control.
>
> —ANNE. L. BARSTOW

To truly transform yourself from a Nice Girl to a Strong Woman and leave your Nice Girl image behind, you will need to pump up what I call the four Power C's—confidence, competence, conviction, and courage.

Each of us already possesses these qualities within us, but our upbringing and our personal experiences can weaken our ability to access them or even rob us of these qualities completely. Most women need to pump up the four Power C's for two other reasons as well. First, these qualities are not ones that girls and women are encouraged to express. In fact, we are *discouraged* from expressing them. When you think about it, the four Power C's seem to be associated more with male behavior rather than with female behavior.

Second, for the most part, girls and women have not traditionally valued these qualities as much as they value the three feminine values: cooperation, compassion, and connection. Although these qualities are much-needed in our world (because they give this world its humanity and balance out the masculine values I call the three A's—autonomy, aggression, and action), as we have seen, Nice Girls tend to exhibit extreme versions of cooperation, compassion, and connection, often to their own detriment.

Confidence

Confidence is the quality that enables us to trust ourselves—our intuition, our instincts, our abilities, our ideas, and our opinions. It enables us to move out of ourselves and into the world, trusting that we will be safe and capable and that what we have to offer is of value. A child must have confidence to take those first steps, to proudly show her finger-painted picture to her teacher, to stand up in front of the class at show-and-tell time, to ride her bicycle without the training wheels. If a child has been encouraged, and if her efforts have been rewarded with praise and/or acknowledgment, she will feel confident enough to continue her forays into the world. If her efforts are met with fear on her parents' part or discouragement in the form of criticism, her level of confidence will be lowered.

Throughout a woman's life, her confidence level will go up or down depending on how well she is received by others. But at some point, it is hoped, each woman will reach a stage where her confidence level becomes more stable and is affected less by how others react to her and her offerings and more by what she thinks and how she feels about her own value.

Confidence Builder #1: Discover Your Essence

Generally speaking, we usually consider our body, our personal history, and our emotional makeup to be the most distinctive and unchanging aspects of ourselves and what define and distinguish us from others. In reality, they are only part of who we are. They only define our outer layer.

To build up your confidence, you need to discover that there is another aspect of you not related to your physical characteristics and not defined by your emotions or personality type. It is not a result of your history and conditioning, nor is it affected by your beliefs or opinions. This aspect of you is sometimes referred to as your *true nature*, or your *essence*, because it is the essence of what you are *beneath* your individual history.

The negative messages you received from your parents (spoken and unspoken) became an *overlay* on top of your essence, often hiding it from your awareness. For our purposes, we will use the word *essence* because it has the connotation of going beneath the negative parental messages you received, beneath the inner critic, and beneath your own self-judgment, to discover your true self. *Essence* also refers to the part of you that is most permanent and unchanging—that which is central in defining who you are.

This is how Byron Brown, the author of the wonderful book *Soul without Shame: A Guide to Liberating Yourself from the Judge Within*, defines *essence*:

> The soul's true nature exists most fundamentally as a now-ness; it is a nature that does not depend on the past or the future, nor does it depend on the experience of being a physical body. The more you have a sense of yourself as soul, the more you are aware that who you truly are is not really defined by your body. Neither is it defined by what you have learned or known in the past. Who you are is something much more intimate and immediate and something much more mysterious and harder to define. To be aware of this is to begin to open to the true nature of the soul, your own beingness *now* in your life.

According to Brown, essence manifests itself uniquely in every person, and that uniqueness is inherent in you at birth. It is not achieved, nor can it be destroyed. It is not dependent on your appearance or anything you do or accomplish. You can, however, lose touch with your true nature—or even forget that it exists. Unfortunately, this is true for many of you reading this book.

The belief in the existence of essence means you have qualities or capabilities beyond those learned or instilled in you by your parents and other caretakers. Your essence is made up of what are called *essential qualities*—attributes essential to what is most true in the experience of being human. These qualities include *truth*, *joy*, *compassion*, *will*, *strength*, *awareness*, and *peace*, to name a few. Essential qualities lie deeper than habit, preference, and early conditioning, and they always exist as potentials buried in the unconscious depths of each person.

The ultimate value of who you are is based not on your

attributes—your physical appearance, your IQ, your talents, or your financial success. It on the miraculous fact that you exist and that at your core you are essentially good, wise, and strong.

EXERCISE: HONORING YOUR ESSENTIAL SELF

1. Find a space inside yourself that symbolizes your internal goodness, wisdom, and strength. Using your internal voice, say your own name. Fill up the whole space with your name. Pronounce your name boldly and lovingly and imagine that your name signifies the importance of your existence. Know that there is only one you, that there is no one else like you, that you are unique.

2. Fill your chest with your name so that you begin to feel alive inside. Remind yourself that you are a precious person, because everyone is precious.

Although we all need validation from others, the true source of your self-esteem and your power comes from within. To access your power, you need to stay connected with yourself. You need to develop the habit of going inside and connecting to your inherent strength, goodness, and wisdom. Doing this throughout the day, every day, will not only help you raise your self-esteem but will help you to feel more inner strength and security.

Confidence Builder #2: Shed Your Idealized Self-image and Embrace Who You Really Are

As children, we learned what was required from us to be liked and accepted by our parents. The result was that we became fixated on an ideal but distorted sense of ourselves. This imagined ideal self became an internal image of how we believe we should be so that everything will turn out all right and we will be loved, accepted, and appreciated. This ideal self-image includes personal standards for action, thought, feeling, behavior, appearance, and accomplishment.

The biggest difficulty with pursuing our ideal self-image is that it doesn't work. Although striving for the ideal as children may have brought us parental approval, it did little to give us inner peace. First of all, the strain of constantly comparing ourselves to an ideal is anxiety provoking and exhausting. Second, since it is impossible to reach an ideal, we are bound to fail and thus always find ourselves lacking, deficient, or not good enough. This sets us up to feel shame and guilt. At some point, we need to question just how valid it is to have an ideal when we use it as a way to continually put ourselves down.

EXERCISE: ACCEPT AND EMBRACE YOUR LESS-THAN-IDEAL SELF

1. Write out a description of yourself and make two lists, the first being all your positive qualities, abilities, talents, and areas of growth. The other list will include negative qualities, traits, limits, and bad habits.

2. Read over your list of negative or less-than-perfect qualities. Try to be neutral and simply acknowledge these aspects of yourself without becoming judgmental about them.

3. Now read over your list of positive qualities and really take them in. Allow yourself to feel the pride that comes from acknowledging that you do, in fact, possess these good qualities.

Confidence Builder #3: Get in Touch with Your Power

Nothing makes us feel more confident than getting in touch with our personal power—to feel the incredible intensity of it, to acknowledge the potential within us. Unfortunately, women may become frightened when they first glimpse their power and the potential for both good and evil it encompasses. In fact, many of us become so afraid of our power that we bury it so that we won't have to deal with it.

Now is the time to reclaim your personal power. Start gradually by standing up for what you want and what you believe in. Learn that you don't have to control anyone but yourself to have control over your own life.

EXERCISE: POWERFUL MEMORIES

1. Remember a time when you felt especially powerful—a time when you exceeded your own expectations or a time when you pushed past your limits.

2. Allow yourself to experience this feeling of power. Savor it and allow it to permeate your being.

Our personal power does indeed need to be respected, but it need not be buried for us to contain and control it and use it for good. Start uncovering your power a shovelful at a time, then take time to get used to it before you dig any deeper. Use this positive and powerful statement: I will begin to own my personal power, learn to honor it and use it for good.

Competence

Having a sense of competence means believing we can make things happen for ourselves in the world—that we can master our environment. Unfortunately, acquiring a sense of competence is no simple task if you happen to have been born female.

Children usually learn that they are competent by surpassing their parents' limits and expectations. For example, parents tell their daughter that she is not old enough to walk home from school alone but she convinces them that she is. The next day, she walks home alone, arriving on time, safe and sound. Not only has she surpassed the limits her parents placed on her, but she learned that she is competent. She thought she could walk home alone, she tried it, and she did it.

The girl who thought she could walk home alone was fortunately already confident that she could do it. But she would have had a lot more confidence had her parents had more confidence in her. The girl's parents, by not expecting much from her, put an obstacle in her path that a less confident child would not have been able to overcome.

The biggest help to a child in terms of developing competence are adults who believe in her abilities before she has demonstrated or proven them. Self-esteem grows out of doing those things we weren't too sure of being able to do in the first place. If we have someone who believes in us, who expects that we can, then taking that first step is a lot easier.

When set at reasonable levels, expectations represent the strongest vote of confidence possible for a child. The problem is that parents often have far too few expectations for their daughters. The expectations parents and our culture traditionally have had for boys are those that lead to a far greater sense of competence than do those for girls. Being competent at cooking and cleaning, for example, doesn't really give one a sense of power and control the way competence in athletics does.

Limits also play an important role in the competence levels of girls. The "sugar and spice" view of girls promotes overprotection and the belief that girls should have things done for them rather than learning to do for themselves. A child who is raised this way experiences her parents' competence but not her own.

Competency Builder

In addition to our parents setting limits on what girls can accomplish, women impose their own limits on what they can achieve.

- List three limits you have set for yourself that prevent you from taking risks (for example, "I'm too inexperienced," "I'm too old").
- List three areas of your life in which you feel competent.
- Now think and write about how you can transfer the feelings of competency you feel in these three areas to the areas of your life where you do not feel competent. For example, I feel competent as a writer and as a therapist. An important aspect of both of these roles is doing research—gathering information. But I do not feel competent when it comes to math. For years, I dreaded doing my taxes; in fact, I would almost become paralyzed with fear. But one day, I realized that there is one aspect of doing taxes that I could actually excel in— gathering up my tax information for the year. From that time on, I focused on this aspect of the process to help me get started. Once I did that, I found I could move on to the math part of the process—adding up the amounts—quite easily (with the help of a calculator).

Conviction

Why do women often lack conviction? Why is it so difficult for many of us to take a stand on controversial issues? Why do we often tend to back down in an argument or confrontation, especially with men?

Women and girls have a strong desire not to hurt others. This often impedes their ability to take a stand or even to stand up for themselves. As one student shared in Carol Gilligan's *In a Different Voice*:

Millions of people have to live together peacefully. I personally don't want to hurt other people. That's a real criterion, a main criterion for me. It underlies my sense of justice. It isn't nice to inflict pain. I empathize with anyone in pain. Not hurting others is important in my own private morals. Years ago I would have jumped out of a window not to hurt my boyfriend. That was pathological. Even today, though, I want approval and love, and I don't want enemies.

Another student explained her reluctance to judge others:

My main principle is not hurting other people as long as you aren't going against your own conscience and as long as you remain true to yourself. . . .There are many moral issues, such as abortion, the draft, killing, stealing, monogamy. If something is a controversial issue like these, then I always say it is up to the individual. The individual has to decide and then follow his own conscience. There are no moral absolutes.

Gilligan reported that this reticence about taking stands on controversial issues, and a willingness to make exceptions all the time were echoed repeatedly by other college women. I have also found it to be true with my female clients. Here is what two of them shared with me: "I don't believe in condemning anyone. You just never know why someone behaves the way that they do." "I don't like forcing my beliefs onto others. Everyone has a right to believe what they believe. Who am I to decide what someone else should believe?"

While these are admirable, if not lofty, sentiments, this way of thinking gets women in trouble. If you cannot determine that an action someone took was wrong, hurtful, or inappropriate, how can you take a stand against it? If you can't determine what is right and wrong, how can you establish boundaries? This is especially true for Enlightened Ones.

Many women experience a sense of vulnerability that impedes their ability to take a stand. According to Gilligan, women's reluctance to judge stems from their uncertainty about their right to make moral statements or perhaps from the price for them that such judgment seems to entail. My experience coincides with her conclusions. Many of my women clients are afraid to take a stand for fear of setting themselves up for negative judgments from others.

Many women have another false belief that we haven't discussed yet—that for women to be powerful, they have to act like men. I believe this is another reason for their inability to speak and act with conviction; they fear being viewed as masculine. But women can be strong and powerful and yet not be like men. We don't have to act like men to be strong—we can act like Strong Women.

Women can have power and not abuse that power. We can stand up for ourselves and not be confrontational, arrogant, or belittling. We can assert ourselves and not take power away from others.

Some women also have trouble seeing themselves as powerful people. This is because they have received a lifetime of messages to be modest and sensitive to other people's feelings, and these messages conflict with the image of women as being powerful without arrogance or oppressiveness.

Power and empathy are not mutually exclusive. We can take pride in our feminine qualities of compassion and empathy without making ourselves weak in the process. We can be kind without being a doormat; we can be strong without being insensitive. We can be truthful about our accomplishments without being arrogant. We can assert ourselves with dignity and civility.

Conviction Builder: Learn to Speak with Clarity and Conviction

By speaking up, you will garner more respect from others, whether it is with your romantic partner, your children, or your colleagues at work. Unfortunately, women often complain that they are ignored when they try to communicate their needs and feelings. Phyllis Mendel, an expert on professional communications and the author of *How to Say It for Women*, recommends that women assert themselves by using what she calls the "grammar of power." According to Mendel, using weak language can undermine your message and your attempts to be assertive. Weak language can thwart your ability to command attention and project confidence. On the other hand, by using phrases and sentences that show you mean business, you will force people to pay attention to what you say. She recommends you start by focusing on changing these four weak grammar forms: hedges, tag questions, excessive modifiers, and hypercorrectness.

Hedging. To hedge is to hide behind words or refuse to commit yourself. We all need to hedge at times—when we don't have an answer, when we are buying time—but women may hedge even when they are certain of the answer, often because they want to soften their statements. Women tend to hedge more often than men do, usually because they are concerned about hurting people's feelings. But this causes them to lose credibility. Hedges make them sound as if they doubt their own words. Which of the following hedges do you use?

- I might not be right, but . . .
- I'm not an expert on this, but . . .
- I don't know much about this, but . . .
- This may only be how I feel, but . . .
- I guess my question is . . .
- I'm not sure how strongly I feel about this, but . . .
- I don't mean to, but . . .
- I just . . .

Using tags. A tag is a short question added to the end of a statement or a command. According to Mendell, tags can take three forms: verbal, vocal, and gestural. Common verbal tags include "okay?" "right?" "isn't it?" "are you?" "doesn't she?" "won't you?" Tags can weaken and undermine our statements because they express doubt. Once again, research suggests that women use tags more than men do. Check the following list and notice which tags you tend to use.

- That's a good idea, isn't it?
- I'm going to go to lunch with my friends, okay?
- I want you to come right home from school today, okay?

- This is the best color for the living room, right?

- I'd appreciate it if you'd call before you come over, do you know what I mean?

- I don't think that's the best way to do this, you see what I'm saying?

Why do these tags weaken and undermine the statements? Notice that the first part of the sentence preceding each is a perfectly clear statement of fact. Yet the tags turn them into questions, hinting that they may not be facts at all.

Women also frequently use vocal tags: the lifting of the voice at the end of a statement so that it sounds like a question. For example, "My name is Beverly? I am a therapist? I write self-help books?" Notice how weak this makes me sound, and yet it has become a very common practice among some women.

Gestural tags include shoulder or neck shrugs. No matter how strong you are sounding, if you use gestural tags, your words will be undermined and weakened. They are unconscious ways in which you negate your words.

Courage

We think we know what courage looks like. Often, images of physical courage come to mind—men fighting for their country, women enduring great pain to protect their children. But courage is different for everyone because fear is different for everyone. Generally speaking, though, an act is considered courageous when we know it is the right thing to do but is difficult to do. We are being courageous when we are afraid but we do it anyway.

You are being courageous when you roll up your sleeves and do the right thing for yourself. You are being courageous when you stop making excuses for someone, when you stop complaining and begging for justice. You are being courageous when you stop expecting people to be fair just because you request it, especially after you've allowed them to get away with their behavior for such a long time. You have to take care of yourself—and that takes courage.

Courage Builder #1: Practice Random Acts of Courage

Courage takes practice. The more often you act courageously, the more courageous you will feel. It takes courage to do all of the following:

- Stand up and allow people to disapprove of and be upset with you.

- Stop *asking* people to see you as a person with rights and instead *become* a person who demands respect with her very being.

- Never allow anyone to tell you who you are.

- Admit it if a friend or a partner is being cruel, manipulative, or unkind, and stop pretending he or she has a good reason for this unacceptable behavior.

Courage Builder #2: Ask Yourself the All-Important Questions

There are three questions that will encourage you to be courageous more than almost any others. The first one is "What are the ways in which I forfeit my right to my life?" (You may do this, for example, by avoiding conflict, by being afraid of other people's anger, by complaining instead of acting.)

Courage also comes from being in touch with your feelings and your needs and then standing up for them. Whenever someone tries to pressure or manipulate you into doing something, ask yourself the second and third questions: "What do I really want at this moment?" and "Will this (action/situation) be good for me?"

Once you have the answers to these questions, you can begin to take action.

EXERCISE: ONE A DAY

1. Start by listing the ways that you can exert your courage and stand up for yourself.

2. Now commit to making one courageous action each day.

Courage Builder #3: Take Your Power

As women, we have watched all our lives while others had the power—the power to rule, to dominate, and to abuse. First, it was our parents; then it was the teachers, partners, and work associates in our lives who seemed to have all the power while we sat by and watched them rule. If we were very, very good, sometimes those in power would bestow on us some privilege or another, giving us the feeling of having a little power ourselves, at least temporarily.

But now all that has changed. We can no longer afford to stand idly by waiting for someone to throw us a crumb of acknowledgment or power. We have to learn to take our power instead of expecting someone to give it to us. Think of it this way: any power that is handed to you is probably not worth having. Take your power.

I value your feedback and would appreciate hearing about how this book has affected you. You can e-mail me at beverly@beverlyengel .com or write to me at P.O. Box 6412, Los Osos, CA 93412-6412.

References

Introduction

Faludi, Susan. *Backlash: The Undeclared War against American Women*. New York: Anchor Books, 1992.

Norwood, Robin. *Women Who Love Too Much: When You Keep Wishing and Hoping He'll Change*. New York: Pocket Books, 1985.

3. The Ten False Beliefs That Set Women Up to Be Used and Abused

Gilligan, Carol. *In a Different Voice: Psychological Theory and Women's Development*. Cambridge, MA: Harvard University Press, 1993.

Pipher, Mary. *Reviving Ophelia: Saving the Selves of Adolescent Girls*. New York: G. P. Putnam's Sons, 1994.

Simmons, Rachel. *Odd Girl Out: The Hidden Culture of Aggression in Girls*. New York: Harcourt, 2002.

4. Stop Putting Others' Feelings and Needs ahead of Your Own

Brown, Nina. *Children of the Self-Absorbed: A Grown-Up's Guide to Getting over Narcissistic Parents*. Oakland, CA: New Harbinger Publications, 2001.

Engel, Beverly. *Loving Him without Losing You: How to Stop Disappearing and Start Being Yourself*. New York: John Wiley and Sons, 2000.

Gilligan, *In a Different Voice*.

Mellin, Laurel. *The Pathway: Follow the Road to Health and Happiness*. New York: Regan Books, 2003.

Steinem, Gloria. *Revolution from Within: A Book of Self-Esteem*. Boston: Little, Brown, 1992.

6. Stop Worrying about What Other People Think of You

Koller, Alice. *An Unknown Woman: A Journey of Self-Discovery*. New York: Bantam Books, 1981.

7. Stop Trying to Be Perfect

Engel, Beverly. *Healing Your Emotional Self: A Powerful Program to Help You Raise Your Self-Esteem, Quiet Your Inner Critic, and Overcome Your Shame*. Hoboken, NJ: John Wiley and Sons, 2006.

Gershen, Kaufman. *Shame: The Power of Caring*. Cambridge, MA: Schenkman Publishing Co., 1980.

Gilligan. *In a Different Voice*.

———. *Making the Connection*.

Mellin. *The Pathway*.

9. Start Standing Up for Your Rights

Engel. *The Emotionally Abused Woman*. New York: Fawcett Columbine, 1992.

———. *The Emotionally Abusive Relationship: How to Stop Being Abused and How to Stop Abusing*. New York: John Wiley and Sons, 2000.

———. *Loving Him without Losing You*.

10. Start Expressing Your Anger

Engel, Beverly. *Honor Your Anger: How Transforming Your Anger Style Can Change Your Life*. Hoboken, NJ: John Wiley and Sons, 2003.

Gilligan. *In a Different Voice*.

Simmons. *Odd Girl Out*.

11. Learn How to Handle Conflict

Rosenberg, Marshall B. *Nonviolent Communication: A Language of Life*. Encinitas, CA: PuddleDancer Press, 2003.

Simmons. *Odd Girl Out*.

12. Start Facing the Truth about People

Bancroft, Lundy. *Why Does He Do That?: Inside the Minds of Angry and Controlling Men*. New York: Berkley Books, 2002.

Stout, Martha. *The Sociopath Next Door: The Ruthless versus the Rest of Us*. New York: Broadway Books, 2005.

13. Start Supporting and Protecting Yourself

Herman, Judith. *Trauma and Recovery: The Aftermath of Violence—from Domestic Abuse to Political Terror*. New York: Basic Books, 1992.

14. The Four C's: Developing Confidence, Competence, Conviction, and Courage

Brown, Byron. *Soul without Shame: A Guide to Liberating Yourself from the Judge Within*. Boston: Shambhala, 1999.

Mendel, Phyllis. *How to Say It for Women: Communicating with Confidence and Power Using the Language of Success*. New York: Prentice Hall, 2001.

Index